Designing and plant garden ponds

D0516843

Part 1
Planning and building

Before you begin digging the hole for your pond, several points must be carefully considered; for example, choosing the right position and deciding on the size of the pond. The first part of this guide covers all of these important details as well as the actual building of the pond. Clear illustrations and precise instructions ensure that the foundation work you do will produce a successful pond.

Part 2
Stylish designs

In this section you will find a host of good ideas for the design of the edge of the pond, as well as additional features such as walkways, bridges, fountains, plant islands, marginal beds and installing useful equipment such as a soakaway or a water filter. Ideas for designs and exact details on how to create them are included.

Part 3
Correct planting

A garden pond without plants would be bleak indeed. Not only are plants attractive but they are also vital for the life of the pond itself. The third part of this guide tells you how to ensure that your plants thrive and gives information about their requirements with respect to position, light, soil or depth of planting as well as how to plant and care for them.

Part 4
Care and over-wintering

The best thing about a garden pond is that it does not involve a great deal of work when considered over an entire year. The fourth part of this book supplies information about ensuring the quality of the water and how to make fish feel at home in the pond. Information and tips on overwintering your garden pond are included.

Only a properly designed pond will give you pleasure.

A stylish pond will greatly enhance your garden.

Plants are both useful and beautiful additions to your pond.

The right care will keep your pond in the optimum state of health.

Introduction

Contents

Sitting beside a pond, admiring water lilies and watching the flight of dragonflies is a very special experience for most people but there is no reason why you should not be able to create such an oasis of peace and relaxation in your own garden. In this guide experienced pond expert Peter Stadelmann demonstrates that building a pond is not as difficult as you may have thought, even if you are having a go for the very first time. The author gives advice on planning and then outlines the building of the pond in a way that is very easy to follow. Step-by-step illustrations are used to show all the work involved. Comprehensive tables will help you to choose the right plants for the conditions in each part of your pond. Fish make a wonderful addition to a pond and you will find valuable information on their choice and care. There is also information on successful overwintering to ensure that your pond survives the coldest season of the year. Lovely colour photographs show spendidly planted garden ponds and lively streams with waterfalls, spring stones and fountains.

The four zones of a garden pond.

Flagstones along the bank.

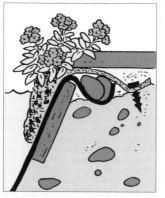

A steep bank with verge matting.

The author
Peter Stadelmann is an
experienced gardener who
specializes in the planning,
building and planting of garden
ponds and streams in the
garden. He is the author of
several garden pond books and
is an aquarium retailer as well
as an instructor and inspector
of aquarium retail traders. He
works with his local Chamber of
Commerce and Industry in
Nürnberg.

The photographers
The photographs in this volume
were taken by Jurgen Becker,
Friedrich Strauss and other
well-known nature
photographers.

The illustrator
Renate Holzner lives and works
in Regensberg as a freelance
illustrator and graphic artist.
Her wide repertoire ranges from
line drawings through photo-
realistic iluustrations to
computer graphics. Her clients
include many well-known
publishers and agencies.

NB: Please read the Author's
Notes on page 60 in order that
your enjoyment of garden
ponds may remain unspoiled.

Planning and building

Good planning is the key to success. So, before you even think about driving your spade into the soil, you must consider various important issues; for example, the right position and the size of the pond. Both the planning and the actual building of the pond require sufficient time. The best way to create a properly functioning pond is described in the following pages.

Above: Iris kaempferi "Embosed".
Left: A properly built pond will soon become an enchanted oasis of peace and tranquillity.

5

Planning and building

Who is going to dig the pond?

This decision is just as important as working out the best place to put a pond in your garden.

Using a spade to dig out a garden pond is a job requiring strength and plenty of energy and it should not be underestimated, particularly if you are not used to hard physical labour. Blisters on your hands, muscular aches and pains or even health-threatening backache and injury can only be avoided if you divide up the digging work in such a way that none of the stages ever overtaxes your strength. The same goes for helpful friends and neighbours!

Hiring a small excavator (and operator) means that the rough work will be done quickly and you can conserve your energy for the careful modelling of the different zones of the pond. You will only be able to use an excavator if there is a suitable means of access for it. The operation will not be cheap either, so make sure you make enquiries at a few firms about a suitable type of excavator, plus prices etc. before you commit yourself.

Disposing of the excavated soil

You should not leave this decision until the soil is lying in a great mound in your garden. Before beginning to dig you should have worked out exactly what to do with the excavated soil.

Most of it can be reused in the garden; for example, for building a protective wall against the weather or for building a waterfall (see p. 31).

Transporting excavated soil can become quite expensive if you cannot get permission to take it to the nearest tip. You may have to take the soil to a special collection and disposal point and will be able to find out about this from your local council.

My tip: Even if the excavated soil is going to be deposited only temporarily on your lawn, before starting you should cover the grass with a large sheet of polythene to avoid damaging the lawn. If you are intending to reuse the excavated soil in your garden, stack grass sods, topsoil and subsoil separately from each other on individual plastic sheets.

Choosing the position

Use the following requirements to find the right position for your pond.

Sunlight: The ideal would be six to eight hours per day. If there is intense exposure to sunlight all day long, plan some space for shade-providing plants (hedges, tall plants along the edges).

Protection from weather: This will be necessary along the sides that receive the harshest weather (north and north west). The house, tall plantings or an earthen bank (made from the excavated soil) will all provide protection.

Trees: If at all possible, do not build a pond under trees; falling leaves in the autumn may drastically lower the quality of the water.

Soil consistency: Some sample digging will provide information on this aspect. A "raised" pond is recommended for a very rocky subterrain (see p. 27).

Mark out the shape when checking the position.

The size of the pond

I am often asked about the minimum size for a garden pond but I can never answer this question by giving a figure in square metres. A small pond may function just as well as a large pond. It will always depend on how it is built and equipped with plants and later looked after. More factors than simply the area will play a part. On the one hand, you may have very definite ideas of your own but, on the other, you will have to consider the well-being of pond inhabitants, both plants and animals, later on. The better you are able to balance your own wishes with practical reality, the more enjoyment you are guaranteed to get from your pond. You will definitely arrive at a suitable solution if you include the following factors in your considerations.

Size of garden: Check whether you have a suitable position for your pond.

● Measure the amount of maximum available space you can give the pond.

● Above all, if you want to have a large variety of plants and creatures, including fish, in your pond, the points given in the panel above should be considered when making a decision on the size of the pond.

The zones of a pond

A garden pond should be built in steps or in a shallow bowl shape with a gentle slope at an angle of about 45 degrees so that four different zones are created.

1 Marginal zone: The area along the edge or bank with a depth of 0-15 cm (0-6 in). If your chosen plants can cope with waterlogging, fill the zone with a 10 cm (4 in) layer of bottom soil; if not, fill the marginal zone up completely with soil.

2 Shallow-water zone: With a depth of water of 15-30 cm (6-12 in).

3 Water-lily zone: Many water-lily types will flourish in this zone which may be up to 60 cm (24 in) deep.

4 Deep-water zone: The depth should be at least 70 cm (28 in) if fish are to overwinter in the pond.

My tip: Among your other considerations beforehand, do not forget to think about a few alternatives to a "normal" garden pond; for example, two small ponds that could be connected by a running stream, a basin with a fountain, or a marginal or marsh bed. Many such possibilities could be incorporated alone or in conjunction with a pond.

Biological zones: A pond is not simply a pit with vertical walls but should have zones containing different depths of water. Only in this way will you create the different biological zones that are necessary to meet the requirements of position for pond plants as well as the vital conditions for pond creatures.

Planning and building

The larger the pond, the more extensive the various biological zones will be. You could save space by having the deep-water zone end in a steep bank but do be careful as there is an increased risk of accidents involving small children. Furthermore, a means of climbing out of the pond should be provided for animals (see safety suggestions, p. 11).

NB: A connection exists between the size of the pond and its biological equilibrium.

Size and biological equilibrium

The size of the pond is not simply a matter of available space as there is also an intimate connection between the size of the pond and the biological activities that go on within it.

Creating biological equilibrium: The aim of all your efforts during building, planting and care is to attain this equilibrium in the pond and to maintain it. This means that a balance has to be maintained between nutrient suppliers (dead and decayed plants/dead creatures) and nutrient consumers (living plants/creatures that prey on plants or other creatures). If more nutrients are produced than are consumed, the quality of the water will deteriorate. The worst scenario is a complete collapse of the pond equilibrium.

A small pond (less than 6 m² /65 sq ft): Biological equilibrium is more difficult to maintain in small bodies of water than in large ones as an excessive supply of nutrients will more rapidly lead to a worsening quality of the water. This means that you are unlikely to manage without some form of technical aid in a small pond that is stocked with a large variety of plants, fish or other creatures. Frequent checks will be necessary so that you are able to respond rapidly if, for example, a large quantity of autumn leaves or a broken filter endangers the biologial balance.

Larger ponds (more than 6 m² /65 sq ft): The larger the pond the less worry there is over the biological equilibrium, provided the pond is properly planned and built and then correctly planted.

Depth of water

Varying depths of water are required to make a pond really suitable as a biosphere for creatures and plants.

The illustration demonstrating different zones (p. 7) gives a guide on depths. (A centimetre more or less will not make much difference.) If fish are intended to overwinter in the pond, it is absolutely essential to have a 1 m² (11 sq ft) area of water that is at least 70 cm (28 in) deep.

Calculation of depth: The depth referred to is the distance between the surface of the pond and the liner or the surface of the medium in a planting basket. This means that if an area of the pond is intended to be 70 cm (28 in) deep but you have covered the floor of the pond with a 10 cm (4 in) layer of material, then you are left with an area that is only 60 cm (24 in) deep. This, in turn, means that you will have to dig the pit 10 cm (4 in) deeper in the first place.

Nature or ornamental pond

Do you wish to have frogs, newts or other amphibians in your pond or do you want goldfish or koi shimmering in the sunlight, water lilies opening their beautiful petals and a gently splashing fountain in the centre? You may, of course, have all of these things but not all together in one pond. Only if you take note of the different biological requirements of creatures and plants when designing and building your pond, will a harmonious community of different life forms be able to thrive there.

Ornamental pond: This usually suggests that fish and decorative plants will be prominent, so please consider the following points.

A pond with a protective grid. Plan enough room for a luxuriant planting around the edges.

A new ready-made pond.

● Ornamental fish require clear, oxygen-rich water. A filter and additional oxygen (see p. 13) will usually be necessary. The fish will require a larger area of water in a pond.

● If you want wild creatures to colonise and establish themselves in your pond, you will have to create special zones, such as a marginal zone and a shallow-water zone, that are inaccessible for fish of any size.

In a nature pond, nature has the final word. Large, natural ponds (15 m² /160 sq ft or more) can be left to their own devices for most of the time. In the case of small ponds, however, a few measures of care will become necessary (see p. 50) or there may be problems with the quality of the water.

Planning and building

Buying a liner

Even if you have to watch the pennies when planning your new pond, you should not stint on one feature – do not try to save money when it comes to the liner.

Quality: Buy only special garden pond liner as manufactured by a range of experienced liner manufacturers. These manufacturers will guarantee all the qualities that distinguish a good liner with a life expectancy of many years. For example, the guarantee should include imperviousness to ultra-violet radiation, resistance to roots, that it will not tear, is impervious to heat and frost and does not contain any substances that could harm animals or plants.

Thickness of the liner: I recommend a thickness of 0.8-1.0 mm. The liner should on no account be thinner than 0.6 mm.

Colour of liner: The usual colours in the trade are black, grey, olive green and brown.

Size: The size should be worked out before buying (see right).

My tip: Leave joining the lengths of liner to the manufacturer or supplier. The handling of liner adhesives requires expert knowledge and is not entirely without risk for a layperson. Damage to health may occur if the adhesive is not handled in the proper way.

Calculating the area of liner required

1 Calculation

Even before you dig the pit for the pond, you can work out how much liner you will need. You will only need to mark out the shape of the pond and its maximum length and width. How to calculate this is shown in the following example for a pond with a surface area of 6 m² (65 sq ft) and a deep water zone that is 70 cm (28 in) deep:

Step 1

Maximum length of pond	3 m (120 in)
+ 2 x depth of water (2 x 70 cm/28 in)	1.4 m (56 in)
+ overlap around edge for fixing liner in position and forming a sill	1 m (40 in)
equals length of liner:	5.4 m (216 in)

Step 2

Maximum width of pond	2 m (80 in)
+ 2 x depth of water (2 x 70 cm/28 in)	1.4 m (56 in)
+ overlap	1 m (40 in)
equals width of liner:	4.4 m (176 in)

2 Measuring

Once the pit has been dug, you can work out the required amount of liner in m² /sq ft as follows. Lay a garden hose or string along the longest part of the pit, measure the length of hose or string, add 1 m (40 in), jot down the figure and do the same for the widest part of the hole.

Buying a ready-made pond

There are countless variations on offer in the trade. Among the features offered are the four biological zones (see p. 7) created by steps.

Sizes of ready-made ponds: The largest choice is usually among ponds up to 8 m (86 sq ft). You may also be able to obtain kits to build large ponds that incorporate streams.

Transporting: Depending on the size of the planned pond, the ready-made pond (and its liner) may be extremely heavy and very awkward to handle. If you do not happen to have strong helpers on the spot, it is a better idea to have the liner or the ready-made pond delivered to your house.

Safety for children

The simple instruction: "You are not allowed to play by the pond" will not be sufficient to extinguish the almost magical attraction that water has for any child. The very youngest ones will not understand the danger anyway and even the most obedient among the older ones will simply forget it. The only thing to do with little children is to make sure that the garden pond is made child-proof right from the start and then still to watch over the children all the time. Such safety precautions will have to be maintained until you are quite sure that there is no more danger to your children. As a rule, even a very gently sloping bank would not be safe as a small child may drown in only a few centimetres of water.

Fences

A fence should be at least 60 cm (2 ft) high and absolutely rigid. It is a good idea to let plenty of greenery grow on the fence; for example, mint, lemon balm, sweet peas, roses, grapevine or runner beans. The plants will make the fence more attractive and also prevent children, who love climbing, from trying to scale it.

Wooden fence: A wooden fence should have vertical battens that are rounded at the top.

Wire-mesh fence: Use galvanized or plastic-coated wire mesh. Metal clips are used to fix the wire to angled posts.

My tip: You will be able to obtain all the necessary materials, as well as advice on building a fence, in a good builders' yard or DIY centre.

Safety grid

A horizontal grid installed about 10 cm (4 in) below the surface of the water is a practical and almost invisible protective measure for smaller ponds, provided, of course, that the grid is installed in such away that it will carry weight and will not tip over. Do remember, however, that a child can still drown in a few centimetres of water.

You will need a soldered, plastic-coated or galvanized builders' steel grid (mesh 6-8 cm/2-3 in wide).

The grid will lie in the pond on top of bricks or U-shaped blocks that are unable to tip or slide. Use flagstones or extra bricks to overcome the problem of varying depths of water.

NB: Always insert pieces of liner beneath any stones placed on the bottom to prevent the actual pond liner from being damaged.

My tip: In the case of smaller ponds that are reinforced around the edges with round blocks of wood, you can fix a net to the blocks (see pp. 9 and 13) using strong, screw-in hooks, or into the soil by means of long tent pegs.

Your legal responsibilities

It is not only the safety of your own children that you must consider. In certain cases, safety measures to protect other people may also be required.

Protecting the general public: As a property owner you have a general duty to protect other persons who do not live on the property, in particular, children. This means that every property owner or tenant should install effective, permanent safety measures to protect children from the results of their own inexperience and lack of thought if it is known that children constantly use the property for play and that they are, therefore, at risk. If your garden pond is situated in a fenced-off section of the garden, you are probably able to assume that unauthorised persons will not trespass on the property. However, you should still do all you can to prevent accidents or, worse, a tragedy.

Planning and building

If, however, the pond is situated in an unfenced front garden or if you are aware that people continually intrude into the area, you will have to take all necessary precautions – within reason – to install safety measures, particularly for the protection of children.

Insurance: Taking out third party insurance is definitely recommended in any case. Ask your insurance company to give you written confirmation that the garden pond is included in the coverage.

Liability for damage by water

In principle, the person (property owner or tenant) who installed the garden pond with its water supply and/or drainage is liable for water damage. For example, if a neighbouring property is flooded or undermined through a malfunctioning water supply line or through incorrect drainage of the pond water, the responsible person will be liable.

Different types of pump.

A pot filter is placed in the pond.

An oxygenator for supplying oxygen.

Safety tips when buying equipment

The handling of electricity in conjunction with water by inexperienced persons can lead to highly dangerous accidents. For this reason, please observe the following safety advice.

● Make sure that a professional electrician carries out all electrical installation work.

● Only buy equipment that carries the British Standard kitemark.

● Never, ever use extension leads! If the cable supplied with the equipment is not long enough, you must have a professional electrician affix a sufficiently long cable.

● Always remove the plug from its socket before removing an electrical appliance from water.

● Only ever allow an expert to carry out repairs.

● Have a fail-safe switch built into your fuse box if there is not already one there. If this is not possible, insert a fail-safe switch between the source of current and the appliance (see photograph, p. 13).

NB: At the time of purchase, make sure that the appliance is safe to use outside.

Liability in the case of accidents involving electricity

In the event of injury, the person who carried out the electrical installation or the owner of the equipment is liable. In all cases, it is extremely important that you obtain liability insurance that specifically includes the pond and stream (if present).

Filters

There are a number of different filter systems, some of which are installed in the pond and others outside it. The pump and filter may be in the form of a single unit or the filter may be run on a separate pump.

It is important to have a filter for a small pond if fish live in the pond.

All filters provide *a mechanical cleaning function*. A filtering material (granules or sponges, for example) filters out larger particles of dirt. Regularly washing out the filter material with clear water will ensure that the pond water remains clean.

A biological cleaning function is provided by all filter systems that have filter materials which, because of their special construction, harbour colonies of micro-organisms. These organisms are able to utilise organic matter (like dead plant matter, food residue) and convert

A fail-safe switch.

Safety net.

it into nutrients for water plants.

NB: It is beyond the scope of this volume to deal with the function, advantages and disadvantages of the many types of filters available on the market. Individual advice and information should be provided if you buy your filter from a good aquarium supplier or specialist garden centre.

Water pumps

The right pump for your pond can be found quite easily in a specialist retailers (aquarium or garden centre). The range of water pumps on the market, which can be used for the most diverse purposes, such as running a filter, for fountains or streams, is so extensive that you will not get very far without some kind of advice. When buying a pump, mention the size of your pond and the purpose of the pump.

Pump stand: This stand can be regulated up to an angle of 35 degrees and can be fixed firmly to an uneven or sloping pond floor.

Equipment for pond care

An oxygenator is a reliable appliance for supplying additional oxygen. It can be left in the pond all year round and is particularly recommended for overwintering (see p. 56).

An ice-preventing device is a simple appliance made of polystyrene and is an ideal overwintering aid (see p. 56).

Pond clippers with 120 cm (4 ft) long handles will help with plant care.

A net with a long handle is practical for fishing out leaves and algae.

Building a pond

A flexible liner for sealing the pond floor or a rigid ready-made pond base are the two best tried and tested methods for creating a pond. These practical pages will explain all you need to know about building a lined pond or installing a ready-made pond.

Building a lined pond

First, mark out the desired shape of the pond with the help of a garden hose (see illustration, p. 6) or with

1 Adjusting the edge of the pond: The edges of the pond will be level if the water level in two PVC tubes attached to the ends of a hose are also at the same level.

small wooden pegs. Dig out a pit and remove all objects with sharp corners or edges (nails, stones, builders' rubble, etc).
Protective layer: If the bottom is very coarse and lumpy, it is worth lining the pond pit with a protective layer of fabric (from the specialist trade). This will protect the actual liner from damage from below.

Adjusting the edge of the pond
(Illustration 1)
Check whether the edges of the pond are level as, if they are not, the pond water may run out of the pit like liquid from a soup plate held on a slant.
A garden hose used as a level is a simple method of doing this. Insert a transparent PVC tube (obtainable at an aquarium suppliers) into each end of the garden hose. Fill the hose with water. Tie one end of the hose to a post set in the pond pit and, holding the other end, walk all around the prospective pond.

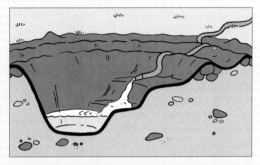

2 Placing the liner in the pond: Allow water to run in slowly and then fix the liner around the edges.

Check that the water levels remain equal. Mark the edge with little wooden pegs. Now make any necessary corrections by adding extra soil or digging some out.

Placing the liner in the pit
(Illustration 2)
Once the edges of the pond are horizontal and all the planned biological zones are marked out, you can lay the liner in the pit. Now allow water to run in slowly until the pond is three quarters full. While the water is running in, you can smooth out wrinkles in the liner or rearrange them in such a way that they are not so noticeable (wrinkles will not harm the liner).

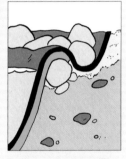

3 Fixing the liner: The edges of the liner must point upwards.

Fixing the liner
(Illustration 3)
Irrespective of how you wish to design the edge of the pond, the important thing is to arrange the liner in such a way that the edges of the material point upwards. This will ensure that the adjacent garden soil does not absorb water from the pond (see p. 18).

Installing a ready-made pond

The following items will be needed for installing a ready-made pond: a spade, a shovel, a trowel, a spirit level, a long, strong plank, a plumb line and a garden hose.

Materials: Dry sand for filling any spaces under the moulded pond (obtainable from a builders' yard). The quantity will depend on the size of the pond.

Marking out the pond pit

(Illustration 4)
If you do not have a template of the shape of the pond, place the pond, open side up, in the required position. Support it in such a way that the edges are horizontal. Now use the plumb line to mark out

(with stones or a string) the outline of the pond on the ground. Add 30 cm (12 in) all the way round so that you will have room to wash sand underneath the mould.

Placing the ready-made pond in the ground

(Illustration 5)
● First dig out the hole for the deepest section of the pond, then dig out the rest of the soil within the marked shape.
NB: The pond pit should be 15 cm (6 in) wider and 5-10 cm (2-4 in) deeper than the respective bays and bulges of the mould.
● Cover the floor of the deepest part of the pit with a 5-10 cm (2-4 in) layer of sand. Pat this layer level with a trowel or short plank.
● Do the same with all

5 Insert the precast pond: Make sure it is level and wash sand and water underneath.

the remaining horizontal areas of the pond pit.
● Lift the mould into the pit, making sure the top edges are horizontal. A thick plank standing on its edge and a spirit level will help you with this procedure.
Washing in sand: All of the hollow spaces underneath the mould should be filled with sand so that the pond does not later sink or tilt.
● First fill all the spaces around the deepest bay with sand. Press the sand down firmly.
● Then fill the mould with water.
● Now, slowly let water run on to the sand layer so that it soaks in and packs the sand down.
● Finally, alternately pack the sand and let water run slowly into all the hollow spaces.

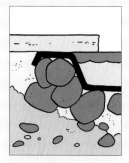

6 A walkable edge: Support the edge with piled up stones.

A path around the edge of the pond

(Illustration 6)
The edge of a path should be supported underneath by stones. First wash sand into the deepest zone, then pack down the stones(if necessary, widen the pit slightly) and continue washing in sand.

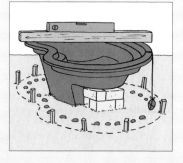

4 Mark out the shape of the pond: Support the basin and use a plumb line and stones to mark out the shape. Add 30 cm (12 in) all the way round.

Stylish designs

Once the pond pit has been dug out and lined, it is time to design the look of the pond. There are as many possibilities for creating an attractive border around the pond as there are for adding decorative features; for example, with walkways, bridges, plant islands, marginal beds or useful installations like a soakaway or a water-cleaning device.

Above: Sundew - a decorative plant for a marginal bed.
Left: A garden pond with a wooden walkway along the bank.

Designing the pond edge

There are many ways of designing the edges of the pond with wood or stone. A practical solution is to construct part of the bank in such a way that you can walk on it. The other parts that are not for walking on can then become an undisturbed space for plants and animals.

Flagstones for a path
(Illustration 1)
A quick and simple solution is to design a walkable edge to your pond using flagstones or patio tiles. For reinforcing the bank, you will need stones that are covered with fabric to prevent damage to the pond liner. The liner can be drawn up over the stones and buried in the soil with its outer edge pointing upwards. Either lay a protective layer of fabric between the flagstones or spread a 5 cm (2 in) thick layer of sand underneath them.

A wooden walkway
(Illustration 2)
A wooden walkway along the bank of a pond is very decorative. Assembling ready-made segments makes the whole job easier to carry out (obtainable from a DIY centre). If you want to build the walkway

3 A path of round wooden blocks can be laid along the edge of the pond on a sand or gravel bed.

1 Flagstones on a bank.

yourself, you should proceed in the following way.
● Dig out soil along the bank to a depth of about 25 cm (10 in) and to correspond with the desired length and width of the walkway.
● Spread a 10-15 cm (4-6 in) thick layer of gravel on top.
● Place three rows of limestone blocks per metre on top of the

gravel layer. Fill the spaces between the stones with sand.
● Place a beam of wood on each of the stone rows. Fix the walkway planks to this beam by means of galvanized nails or screws.
● Nail the pond liner to the front beam and cover it with a wooden pelmet.

Wooden paving
(Illustration 3)
A "pavement" made out of rounds of wood makes a very decorative walkable edge to a pond. The rounds can be bought ready made in a timber yard or builders' yard. They should be laid on a bed of gravel or sand.
The paving bed: The pond liner should not yet

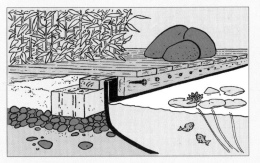

2 A wooden walkway built along the side of the pond requires a stable foundation.

4 A small marginal bed along the edge of a pond can be planted with a wealth of greenery.

be fixed to the edge. If necessary dig up the edge of the liner.

The entire area to be "paved" needs digging out to a depth of about 15 cm (6 in) to make the bed. Now fill the excavated area with a layer of sand or gravel about 15 cm (6 in) thick. Draw the liner over medium-sized stones and lay it in such a way that the edge of the liner will stick up between the first and second rows of wood blocks. Protect the liner from damage by sprinkling a thin layer of sand around the area of the first row of blocks or lay a protective layer of fabric on top.

Installing the "paving": Embed the wooden blocks, jammed tightly against each other, in the sand or gravel bed.

Tap the blocks down lightly and spread sand over the tops of the blocks with the help of a coarse broom until all the spaces between the blocks are filled. Cover the edge of any liner that may protrude along the edge with gravel.

A small marginal ditch

(Illustration 4)
The part of the pond's edge that is not to be walked on can be enhanced with a marginal ditch.

● Dig a trench about 30-40 cm (12-16 in) wide along the edge of the pond so that the water in the ditch will be at the same level as the water in the pond.

● Lay liner in this section of ditch so that the edge of the liner points upwards.

● Cover the edge of the ditch nearer to the pond with stones. If necessary, glue heavy stones into position with a silicon adhesive so that they cannot tip over.

● Fill the ditch with soil and plant marginal plants that do not like waterlogging.

Building a steep bank

(Illustrations 5 and 6)
Steep banks need to be secured; for example, with large stones (see illustration 5) or with a drystone wall of stones piled on top of each other. These stones are not cemented together (see illustration 6).

Verge matting with integral planting pockets is ideal for planting along steep banks. The matting should be anchored into the soil behind the liner. Special fixing hooks can be obtained for the purpose.

My tip: A cat with fishing ambitions can be foiled if you lay flagstones in such a way that they protrude about 20 cm (8 in) over the edge of the water (cement the stones in at the edge!).

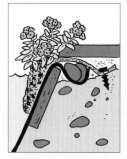

5 A steep bank with verge matting.

6 Flagstones that protrude about 20 cm (8 in) over the water will make pondlife safer from cats.

Stylish designs

Using stone

Stones have always been an indispensable item of design in the garden and around the house and they constitute a valuable building material. They are an important building and decorating accessory for the pond builder also.

Suitable types of stone that can be utilized in a problem-free way in and around a pond are all basic stones like large river pebbles or boulders, different-coloured slate, sandstone, lava and basalt. None of these stones release substances that might impair the quality of the water.

Unsuitable stone: Limestones that are eroded by rain and which would release "water hardeners" into their environment. If such substances end up in the pond, they might well have a detrimental effect on the water.

Stones and their use

When we speak of stones, we generally think first of decorative types of stone but there are also some that are not so attractive but, nevertheless, are still extremely useful for building a pond.

Pebbles and other natural stones are used for reinforcing the banks of the pond and for designing the edges. It is easy to draw a liner over gravel or

pebbles at the edge of the pond (see p. 14) and hide it under an attractive stone wall.

Chunks of natural stone are ideal for building a drystone wall that can be used to support and reinforce steep banks or sloping sides.

Perforated bricks are manufactured for house building but I can recommend them highly as a universally employable aid for pond building. For example, it is quite simple to build up a quick layer as a boundary between a marginal and shallow-water zone and also to build plinths for water-lily baskets or a pump.

My tip: Make sure that the openings of the perforated bricks are sideways on so that the water can flow through.

L- and U-shaped stones are building blocks moulded out of concrete, which are used for building houses and roads. This should not deter you, as L-shaped stones are unbeatable as supporting elements for steep banks, slopes or ponds with raised water levels (see pp. 26/27). The U-shaped stones make excellent, stable foundations for paving stones, for example.

Paving stones and flagstones

There are endless possibilities for designing the edge of the pond with paving stones or flagstones. A narrow strip, forming a path round the pond, or a whole paved area for a table and chairs will look good if made out of decorative stones.

Paving: Paved areas made of natural stone, concrete or clinker should be laid so that they are impermeable to water and virtually indestructable. The most beautiful patterns can be laid down although the more complicated ones are best left to an expert. Simple patterns are easy enough for the layperson (see p. 18).

Flagstones: Paving slabs made of natural stone or concrete and intended for use on paths or patios come in many decorative variations. The selection is enormous although the simplest, most natural-looking ones are the best choice for the edge of a pond, particularly if larger areas are to be covered. All stone paving slabs require a stable foundation. Along flat banks, large stones will be sufficient but steep banks require a drystone wall as a foundation.

My tip: Do not use flagstones with a very smooth surface around ponds. When they get wet or icy, they can become very slippery indeed.

There are many attractive possibilities for designing the edge of the pond with stones and wood.

Tips on buying stones

Large pieces of dressed stone in all sizes and the very useful perforated bricks and L- and U-shaped stones can all be obtained from most builders' yards.

In the case of natural stones, finding the right ones may be a little more difficult. In some areas you may find specialist natural-stone retailers (try *Yellow Pages* or your local business telephone directory). As the transport costs for stones can be high, you should try to find a supplier who is as near as possible.

NB: Stones that are found lying around in the landscape will always belong to someone. This means that you will only be entitled to remove them after obtaining permission to do so.

Using wood

Most gardens these days contain features made of wood. Wood fits as harmoniously as stone into the general garden scheme, looks natural and is usually easy to work with even for the layperson.

When building a pond, wood is excellent as both a design feature and a useful element.

Stylish designs

Wood for the garden: Many builders' yards offer a wide range of round wood, square-cut wood, planks for paths and much more. This type of wood is, as a rule, pressure treated which means it will have a long life even if it is in constant contact with soil. If you are going to use wood around your pond, you should make sure to ask for pressure-treated wood as it is most suitable for this purpose.

Unsuitable wood: I do not recommend cheap building wood as it usually decays rather quickly. On no account should you use old railway sleepers as they are sure to be contaminated with oil and herbicides. If these substances are washed into the pond water through the action of rain, both the water and the life in the pond will be poisoned.

Tips on the use of wood

Rounded wood and square-cut wood driven vertically into the pond bank serve two purposes: the portion of the wood that ends up in the soil will form a stable bank fortification and the part above ground makes a decorative walkway around your pond.

Wooden sections also make good supports when laying the course of a stream (see p. 34) or for a pond on a slope.

My tip: Even if you do use the best quality wood in the garden,

Installing an overflow

After heavy rain, the pond may be in danger of flooding its banks but a soakaway will serve as a drainage or overflow point. A simple solution is to use a composting basket (obtainable in the garden trade). Dig a hole the same size as the basket, line the walls but not the bottom of the basket with liner and fill it with fist-sized stones. Dig a channel between the basket pit and the pond, insert lining material and fill the channel with stones.

A soakaway for the overflow.

you should always insert a sheet of liner between the wood and the pond water. This will also prevent any damaging substances – toxic or not – from being washed into the pond water.

Bridges and walkways

Bridges and walkways belong to the more ambitious school of pond design. They require a lot of work and are not cheap.

Bridges made of wood, natural sandstone or concrete can be bought in many different sizes and designs in the garden or wood specialist trade. The difficulty in building such structures depends on their size and weight. The most important thing is always that the bridge should be supported or fixed at both ends with a stable foundation.

Expert advice, and often the help of a professional builder, are important if you want to be sure of not only a beautiful bridge but also a safe one.

Walkways that can be installed along a bank or even reach out across the pond can be erected by an experienced do-it-yourselfer.

The most important element for both types of walkways is a solid foundation along the bank. Walkways that reach out over the pond have to be supported and shored up safely. One way of doing this is to place two U-shaped blocks, with the two legs upwards, on top of liner pieces and protective fabric in the pond. Stand the support pillars of the walkway in the U-shaped stones and fix them in with concrete. Nail battens crosswise to the pillars for extra stability.

Stepping stones

Stepping stones provide the ideal way of walking through a pond without getting your feet wet. They are particularly useful for very large ponds as they make all measures of care easier.

Use U-shaped stones, perforated bricks glued together with silicon or paving slabs for installing stepping stones of different heights.

My tip: Install stepping stones only in shallow water. Stones that are too high (over 50 cm/ 20 in) may wobble and can be dangerous.

Light around the pond

Floating, globe-shaped lights or decorative lamps along the edge of the pond will provide magical illumination in the garden in the evening and at night.

Recommended: Lamps or lights with an electric current supplied via a transformer that is connected with a normal mains network and which brings the voltage down to 12-24 volts. A transformer should prevent any potentially lethal accidents.

Natural water-cleaning devices

Keeping the pond water clean is not only achieved by employing technical filters, it can also be accomplished with small, environmentally friendly, biological, water-cleaning facilities using plants that will keep the pond water and pondlife in harmony in the most natural way. Such bio-filters are offered in various different models. All aim to ensure that nature's own self-purifying systems, which function to maintain the equilibrium in ponds and lakes, are working at optimal levels.

Installation: These small units, which are sometimes referred to as in-pond filters, are installed in a pit at the edge of the pond. The internal working of the filter depends on the type used. The illustration below shows a model with one chamber, a gravel layer, a filter mat and a sand layer. Planting compost and plant baskets have been installed on top of these.

Plants: Suitable plants are reeds, bulrushes and irises.

Water circulation: This is kept going by means of a hose and a pump. The capacity of the pump should not be more than 5 litres (9 pt) per minute (= 300 litres/66 gal per hour) as the water should just trickle.

Function: While the dirty water is slowly trickling through the filter, all coarser large particles are filtered out. The plants remove nutrients which they require for their growth from the water. In addition, millions of micro-organisms convert organic substances so that they can be utilized by the plants. The clean, oxygen-rich water flows back into the pond.

A water cleaning unit with plants will help to keep the water clean in a natural way.

A pond where people swim must be set apart from the pond in which animals and plants live.

A swimming pond

Very few people have a garden that is large enough for a swimming pool and a garden pond. Furthermore, a shining blue pool looks alien in a nature garden. If the pond is big enough, however, you may still be able to enjoy splashing about in a pond.

Size of pond: 15-20 m² (160-215 sq ft) is essential if you want to use the pond for splashing about. It will need to be a lot larger (about 30-40 m/320-430 sq ft) if you want to do proper swimming.

Depth of pond: 80-150 cm (32-60 in) is ideal for a swimming area.

Design of pond: Obviously, the swimming area and the zone for animals and plants will have to be kept separate from each other.

A pleasant place to sit.

● The simplest version is a loosely layered stone wall or L-shaped stones in a row. Both should end about 20 cm (8 in) beneath the surface of the water so that an exchange of water can take place between the two zones.

● A more elaborate method is to build a basin for the swimming area and then install a wide, flat, sloping bank with a pond adjoining it.

Animals and plants near a bathing area

The larger the biotope zone, the more versatile the animal and plant world that will develop.

Animals: In spite of the separation of the two zones, bathing will create a disturbance in the pond which may induce amphibians, in particular, to take flight. Dragonflies, beetles and other insects will, however, still colonise the biotope zone. If the bathing pool is smaller than 40 m² (430 sq ft), you should not keep fish as their well-being would be severely disturbed.

Planting: You can plant all types of marginal and shallow-water plants in the biotope zone. The bathing zone should contain only water lilies and a few reeds.

Warning: Some species of reeds are as sharp as knives. These species should not be planted in the bathing area! Get expert advice from a specialist retailer.

Care: A good pond filter (switch this off when you are swimming) is important for animals, plants and humans. Also change the water regularly. Every six weeks during the summer, drain off about one third of the pond water and allow an air pump to pump air through the water. Thorough care of your pond in the autumn (see p. 54) will be necessary.

A mini-pond for your patio or garden

Mini-ponds, installed in large containers on your patio or in your front garden, make an attractive feature. A mini-pond of this type will have to be re-started every spring, after the last cold snap of winter. Then set up the pond in a sunny spot where it will be sheltered from wind in the autumn.

Containers: All containers are suitable provided they have a capacity of more than 10 litres (2 gal). Plastic containers should be surrounded with wood to prevent them from heating up too fast in strong sunlight.

Planting: The best plan is to place the plants in small-mesh baskets geared to the size of the container. The best planting compost is aquarium compost (from aquarium suppliers). Fertilize after planting with one tablet of nitrogen fertilizer per basket (obtainable in the specialist trade). Cover the top surface of each

basket with about three fingers' width of fine gravel (particle size 5-7 mm).

Plants: the following plants do well together.

● dwarf water lily, lotus, purple loosestrife (*Lythrum salicaria*), mare's tail (*Hippuris vulgaris*) and creeping Jenny (*Lysimachia nummularia*)

● water fringe (*Nymphoides peltata*), dwarf reed mace (*Typha minima*), water hawthorn (*Aponogeton distachyos*), flowering rush (*Butomus umbellatus*), great spearwort (*Ranunculus lingua*) and hornwort (*Ceratophyllum demersum*)

● dwarf water lilies (*Nymphaea* spp.), umbrella grass (*Cyperus* spp.), water crowfoot (*Ranunculus aquatilis*) and *Elodea*

Plant care: Cut back plants occasionally; the fast-growing ones more often and more rigorously than the slow-growing ones. Make sure the late-flowering ones, like cardinal flower (*Lobelia cardinalis*), do not become smothered by other plants.

Water care: Once a month, exchange one third of the water and add a water preparation agent (follow the manufacturer's instructions on dosage!).

Overwintering: Empty the mini-pond around the middle of autumn. Cut back plants severely and remove all leaves. Place all planting baskets in a large plastic bowl, cover with foliage and stand the bowl in a frost-free position until spring.

Ponds

The following pages describe various types of ponds.

A pond on a slope
(Illustrations 1 and 2)

The most important thing about a pond in a sloping position is that the soil should not start to slip away.

L-shaped blocks (from builders' yards) make excellent reinforcements for both the slope and the valley (lower) sides of a pond.

● Dig out the slope to about 70 cm (28 in) deep. Place the L-shaped stones in a row, packed tightly side by side, with the shorter leg pointing towards the slope. Pile up soil and stones behind them in a sort of dry-walling technique.

● The valley (lower) side can be reinforced with L-shaped stones but, this time, with the shorter leg of each stone pointing away from the slope.

● For safety reasons, shore up the L-shaped stones on the valley side

with a few larger stones.

● As shown in illustration 1, draw the liner over the L-shaped stones.

● Cover the L-shaped stones on the valley side by building a drystone wall with steps.

Rounded wooden blocks (see illustration 2) are also suitable for reinforcing the valley side. The wooden blocks should be sunk into a foundation made of concrete. Fix the liner around the edges by wrapping it around a wooden batten and nailing it, together with the batten, to the rounded blocks.

A plant island
(Illustration 3)

A floating garden with exotic-looking marginal plants is an especially eye-catching feature in a pond. You can build a plant island of this sort yourself and the materials can be obtained from any builders' yard.

You will need: 1 m² (10 ¾ sq ft) of 30 cm

1 A pond on a slope should be built in such a way that the soil cannot slip away.

(12 in) thick polystyrene sheeting, 8 m (27 ft) long squared wooden beams (8 x 10 cm/3 x 4 in wide) (cedar wood is very durable) and four long, non-rusting bolts with nuts.

Building the island: Cut 1.25 cm (½ in) holes into the polystyrene and stuff the holes with peat moss (garden centre). The moss will act like a wick and will later supply the "bed" with

2 Rounded pieces of wood should be sunk into the foundation.

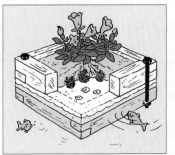

3 An island for marginal plants is easy to build yourself using wooden beams and polystyrene sheeting.

water. Now make two frames (the size of the polystyrene sheet) out of the beams.
Stand one frame on, and the other under, the polystyrene, drill holes into the corners of the frames and polystyrene and join them together with the nuts and bolts.

Planting: Fill the frames with peat (soil is too heavy) and plant marginal plants.

Care: Water only with rainwater if necessary. Never fertilize.

My tip: Anchor the island by means of a large stone tied to a rope.

Marginal bed
(Illustration 4)

If you would prefer to plant your marginal plants on land, you can install a marginal bed

along the bank or somewhere in your garden in a large plastic tub sunk into the ground. Fill with a 5-10 cm (2-4 in) layer of gravel. Stand holed yoghurt containers upside down on the gravel. Use a small, transparent plastic tube as a water level meter. Fill the container with peat and water and plant the marginal plants. Keep the bed very moist with rainwater.

A pond with a raised water level
(Illustrations 5 and 6)

This kind of pond is particularly recommended for gardens with a rocky subsoil. Two ideas are shown in illustrations 5 and 6.

5 A pond with a raised water level for gardens with a rocky sub-terrain.

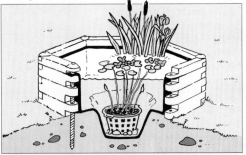

6 A collapsible pond made of wooden elements should stand on a level base.

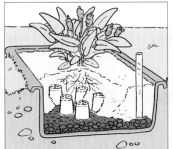

4 A marginal bed with an irrigation system made of plastic cups is quick to build and easy to care for.

Ready made pond: Dig a pit for the deep-water zone only, insert the mould and stabilize the pond all the way round with the help of L-shaped stones so that the edge of the pond mould is resting on the blocks. A wooden pallisade or drystone wall covered in attractive plants will cover up the L-shaped blocks.

Collapsible pond: This type of pond can be purchased in the trade and is made of wooden beams. You can usually choose whatever shape you fancy. The pond is put together with the help of jointed rods. It is clad on the inside with pond liner that is fixed in position under the top beam.

The fascination of running water

For many people, water increases in fascination when it begins to run, bubble and splash, making the drops of water sparkle in the sunlight. Fountains and other devices beside or in a garden pond are just as lovely to look at as water lilies.

Making the water move is not a difficult matter in a garden pond and the range of attractive fountains etc. to choose from is huge (see pp. 30/31). However, do not forget that the garden pond is a habitat for plants, fish and other creatures. Many of them will not cope with water constantly trickling down upon them or if they have to live in persistently agitated water.

Tips on choice: Particularly if the pond is small, you should consider the following points when choosing a fountain or some other device.

● Choose a small fountain for a small pond.

● The more natural the pond is supposed to look, the gentler the splashing of water should be.

● Fountains which create a downpour of water do not belong in the biosphere of a garden pond and should be installed in a separate basin.

A small waterfall in harmony with the surrounding plants.

Moving water

A pond pump provides the moving force for any kind of running water. Trying to choose the right one for your own pond from the wide range of pumps and accessories (jets, bell-shaped water fountains, etc.) requires access to sensible advice and good information when purchasing. The alternatives to electrically operated pumps are the environmentally friendly solar pumps which do not require connection to the mains. The sun will provide the required energy at no cost, with the help of solar panels that are directed towards the sun. An accumulator installed as an energy store will help to keep the water moving, even on dull days.

Spring stones provide a popular form of running water.

A stone basin.

A foam fountain.

A terracotta water spout.

Stylish designs

Spring stones

One of the most popular devices is a spring stone. They can be used in any pond as they keep the water moving very gently. Spring stones can be made out of mill stones or out of natural stones equipped with a central hole (see p. 29). They are on the market in all manner of sizes, made of natural stone or artificial materials.

Installing spring stones: Several possibilities exist, for example:

● They can be integrated into a shallow-water zone.

● They also look good placed in a separate basin at the edge of the pond, so that the water can run into the pond. You will need to dig out a hollow at the edge of the pond, clad it with protective fabric and liner and fill it with large stones.

NB: Complete kits can be obtained in the trade. These include a spring stone, a basin (lined basin or squared wooden basin) and filler material. These basins can be installed at the edge of the pond or placed completely separately somewhere in the garden. Follow the manufacturer's instructions. A submerged pump will keep **the water inlet** clear. It should come with different-shaped jet attachments that can create a small, squirting fountain, for example.

Another possibility: Use the stone for supplying fresh water by passing one end of a hose through the hole in the stone and attaching the other end to the mains.

The hole in the stone: Any large stone can be converted into a spring stone if it is equipped with a hole. I strongly recommend that you do not drill the hole yourself. The harder the stone, the faster your ordinary drill will give up the ghost and break, quite apart from the increased risk of accidents caused by stone fragments flying about. If you should purchase or even find a good stone without a hole in it, leave the hole-making to an expert.

Water spouts

There is a vast range of figures with water spouts. Whatever you are looking for, you are sure to find something suitable in the gardening trade or in the catalogues of specialised manufacturers. From the classic fat-cheeked cherub through diverse animal figures to futuristic sculptures, anything can be bought, made of many different materials such as plastic, ceramic and sandstone.

Please note the following points *when installing* a water-spout figure:

● Stand the figure at the edge of your pond in such a way that it cannot tip over into the pond.

● Always place a piece of protective fabric under the figure to protect the pond liner.

● If the figure is very heavy, support it from below on a plinth of rounded wooden blocks sunk into the soil.

My tip: Do not let the water spout run all the time and also make sure the water spray does not land on water lilies. The best plan is to utilize the water spout to provide a fresh water supply by connecting it to the mains.

Small fountains

It is fascinating to see what beautiful shapes water can be made to create with the help of different pump attachments. These can be used to conduct water in narrow or wide cascades, shaped like a bell or in a wide-spraying water star. Such shapes are very beautiful but they do not belong in every pond. Furthermore, if you want to enjoy undisturbed pond wildlife, you should curb your passion for running water and choose a small fountain that allows a gentle stream of water to flow from no great height. Anything more elaborate should be installed in a separate basin that can be sited at the edge of the pond or in another position in the garden without a great deal of trouble.

A decorative basin with running water will enhance the beauty of your garden.

My tip: Install a small fountain that is driven by a waterpump. Place this on a perforated brick or on a pump stand (see p. 13). This will enable you to place the pump quite easily in the position required for the fountain.

Fountain and basin

This is the largest type of fountain and usually a great favourite. Unfortunately, it is not at all suited to a garden pond. The volume of water that pours down is harmful to water lilies and other water plants and it also affects all other pond inhabitants adversely. In short, a large fountain will only cause trouble in a pond. If you dearly wish a large fountain or any other gushing fountain type, you will have to build a separate water basin for it. The most practical way to install one is to purchase a complete fountain kit of the type offered in most aquarium retailers or in some garden centres. These kits contain everything you will need to create a splendid fountain, namely a lined basin, a pumpshaft with cover, a pump, a fountain attachment and building instructions.

Installing a small waterfall

A small waterfall can be recommended for any pond. Properly installed, its gentle flow and bubbling sound invite one to sit and daydream but will also prove of real benefit to the pond.

The movement of water enriches the pond with oxygen which, in turn, improves the quality of the water.

My tip: If you are planning to install a stream that will flow into the pond, the waterfall described here will be ideal for the end of the stream just before it trickles gently into the pond.

You will need: Three to five step basins made of natural stone or plastic, also soil and gravel.

Method

● Pile up a small heap of soil (excavated soil produced when digging the pond or garden soil) to create the necessary gradient.

● Form steps with the help of a trowel and cover them with a 5-10 cm (2-4 in) layer of gravel as a base for the step basins.

● The basins are set on top. The lowest basin should protrude slightly over the pond.

NB: If you are using ready-made stream or step basins, the waterfall need not be lined with pond liner. If you build the whole thing yourself out of stone slabs, paving stones or natural stones, you will need to seal the course.

Make sure that the pond liner is fixed properly at the edges of the pond (see p. 14).

A small waterfall requires a stepped but not too steep gradient. It can be built quickly using step basins.

Stylish designs

A garden stream

While a stream is attractive and provides an eye-catching feature in any garden, it also provides several important advantages. A slowly flowing stream helps to maintain biological equilibrium as it functions as a biological filter. The prerequisite for this is that the stream flows into the pond and its source is fed with pondwater via a pump and hose. Provided the bed of the stream has been properly installed, the pondwater should flow slowly along the stream allowing the largest particles of detritus to be caught. In addition, micro-organisms (for example, certain bacteria) that colonise a well-functioning stream will convert organic waste into nutrients that are reused by the plants growing in the pond and stream.

NB: If the stream is to fulfil its filtering function, it will have to flow constantly from mid-spring to mid-autumn. If it is switched off for longer than two or three hours, the bacteria will die and the cleaning function will cease almost entirely.

Advantage for the garden: The slightly moister air that is created by running water will help the plants growing on either side of the stream to thrive. Along the banks of the stream, there is plenty of room for several very varied moist biotopes which will provide many creatures with food and shelter.

Length, width and depth of a stream

These three factors depend on the conditions in your garden.

Width of stream: The wider the stream, the more room you will require to install the typical meandering course of a stream. If you start with an average width of 50 cm (20 in), you will be able to build the stream to be both functional and look natural (see p. 34).

Length of stream: There is a handy rule for this. Calculate 1.5 m (5 ft) of stream for every 6 m² (65 sq ft) of pond surface area. A 6 m² (65 sq ft) pond will contain about 4 m³ (140 cubic ft) of water, so the stream should be about 6 m (20 ft) long.

Depth of stream: A stream is not a canal. Varying depths of water are typical for a stream. If you work from an average depth of 25 cm (10 in), the stream will be easy to design (see p. 34).

Gradient

You do not have to own a house on a hillside nor will you have to pile up huge heaps of soil to get your stream to flow. Even a gentle gradient of a few centimetres will permit water to flow.

Basic rules for installing a gradient:

● The source of the stream should be at the highest point of the gradient.

● The gradient should always slope very gradually. If you build the source on a hill and the bed of the stream on the level, the water will plunge like a waterfall into the bed of the stream and wash away all forms of life.

● If the gradient is already quite steep, the stream should be built in steps that will act as small dams. By making them longer or shorter, wider or narrower, you can effectively control the gradient.

● If your property is on a slope, you must dig until you have excavated a bed with the right gradient.

A garden stream makes a beautiful and useful addition to a garden pond.

Dammed steps.

Plants for a stream

A stream can only fulfil its full filtering effect with the help of plants. The materials broken down by the stream's population of micro-organisms produce nutrients that can be utilised by plants. If all of these waste materials ended up in the pond, there would be an excessive build up of nutrients and the result would be increased growth of algae. Do not be too sparing in planting along the edge of the stream, particularly as such plants are not expensive. They will grow vigorously and be effective all the time. The plant tables on pages 42/43 and 46/47 will tell you whether a particular plant is suitable for planting along a stream.

The proper way to build a stream

Building the bed of the stream

The width, depth and course of the bed of the stream should vary on the way from the source to the mouth. Allow the stream to flow in wide, S-shaped loops. Make sure that no acute angles are created, however, or the water will not flow properly and may overflow its banks.

Width: Small bays, dammed zones, wide marginal zones along the banks and planted mesh baskets in the stream bed will ensure that the water flows along slowly.

Depth: An average depth of 25 cm (10 in) will be sufficient. The varying depths typical of streams can be obtained with the help of different heights of dammed steps or by using filling material like stones or gravel.

Sealing the stream with pond liner

I recommend a good pond liner with a thickness of 1 mm.

The amount of liner required should be calculated when the bed of the stream is almost finished. Measure it in the same way as for a garden pond (see p. 10).

Fix the liner to the edges in the same way as for a pond. The liner edges should end up pointing upwards.

Any edges to be walked on should be reinforced. The liner should be drawn across the stones and laid in such a way that its edges are pointing upwards.

Ready-made parts: Stream basins made of different materials that can be used to combine with liner to create short streams are available in the trade. You should also be able to obtain pre-formed, ready-made stream parts that can be installed in the same way as a ready-made pond.

Plant baskets in a stream bed

Plant baskets can be used to vary the width of the stream bed quickly and simply, thereby decreasing the speed of flow of the water:

● Narrow, longish, mesh baskets are well suited to this; they can be filled with nutrient-poor plant compost (sand and clay in equal parts).

● The baskets can be filled with dwarf reed mace, marsh marigold, arrowhead or water mint.

● Alternate the baskets along both sides of the stream so that two baskets are never exactly opposite each other.

1 Sealing the stream: Lay a fabric layer under the liner if the ground is stony.

2 Plant baskets in a stream: Set on alternating sides of the bank, they will regulate the speed of flow of the water.

3 Source and dam steps: These can easily be built with rounded wood blocks and planks.

4 Sealing dammed steps: Draw about 20 cm (8 in) of liner through the overflow opening and cut it in such a way that it lies smoothly against the dam plank. The liner can be fixed to the plank with pins or small tacks.

Steps
(Illustration 3 and 4)

The shallow steps can be securely installed with the help of round wooden blocks or squared wood, beams or battens.

Method
● Mark all steps and peg out their width, length and course.
● Also mark out the height of the support.
● Set the vertical rounded wooden supports close together at the same height.
● Fix horizontal connecting planks to the insides of the vertical sections of wood.
● Now build up the inside of the steps with soil, gravel or wooden

sleepers. The individual step dams may be of varying depths but should always be level.
● A dam plank with a shallow section cut out should form the edge of each step. Insert the plank in the groove between the vertical sections of wood.
● Finally, cover all segments individually with liner and seal off the transitions from one step to the next (see illustration 3).

A marginal zone at the edge of the stream
(Illustration 5)

Additional living space for plants and places to hide for amphibians and other small creatures are provided by the

installation of small marginal zones along the banks. For this purpose, you should extend the stream bed in several places. These areas need not be any deeper than 10-15 cm (4-6 in). The marginal zones should be bordered by stones which will ensure that water flows very slowly and gently through them. Fill up these zones with soil and plant marginal plants.

5 A marginal zone along the bank: Mark it off with stones and fill it with nutrient-poor compost.

Correct planting

A garden pond could not exist without plants. Not only would it be boring but you would not enjoy it for long as the plants are vital to the garden pond biotope. When choosing plants you will need to consider their requirements with respect to position, light, soil and depth of water in order to ensure that they will thrive and flourish.

Above: Water lilies are the most popular pond plants.
Left: An attractive variety of plants in a garden pond.

37

Correct planting

Planning the planting

After you have finished your building work it is time to buy your plants. Garden centres, aquarium retailers and specialist water garden nurseries can provide everything the pond owner could wish for. However, if you start buying as if there were no tomorrow and just have anything that takes your fancy you will be most put out later on when your pond begins to suffocate in a muddled mass of plants. Precisely because the plants will be tiny when you buy them, it is well worth working out what to plant beforehand with paper and pencil, always taking into consideration the varying requirements of the plants in question (see tables, pp. 40-47).

Botanical names

Admittedly, some botanical names are not easy to pronounce but it can be very useful to know them and to use them when purchasing plants. For example, if you simply purchase an "iris", you may have problems as the *Iris kaempferi* (Japanese marsh iris) does not like waterlogging, while *Iris pseudocorus* (marsh or water iris) can grow in water up to 25 cm (10 in) deep.
Unlike the common name of a plant, its botanical name is valid worldwide and consists of at least two descriptive words.
The genus name, for example, *Iris*, comes first and is always given an uppercase letter.
The species name, for example, *kaempferi*, comes second and begins with a lowercase letter.
The complete name is written in italics: *Iris kaempferi*.
Varieties and hybrids are cultivars that are differentiated from the pure species by colour or the shape of the flowers (double, fringed, etc.). They have an additional name which is placed in inverted commas, for example, *Iris kaempferi* "Embosed".

Planting compost

No matter whether you are placing the plants in prepared soil or in a planting container, use only nutrient-poor soil. Nutrient-rich or fertilized soil will encourage algae formation and will have dire consequences for the quality of the water.
A mixture that is very suitable for most pond plants is clay and sand in a ratio of 1:3 or 1:4. Some plants have special requirements (see table, pp. 42/43). They may require slightly acid, that is, lime-free soil. For these, a clay-sand-peat mixture in a ratio of 1:1:1 is suitable. For plants that require very acid soil, the ratio is 3:3:1.
My tip: Plants with special requirements in the marginal zone can be set in planting baskets so that they can still be combined with others.
Special pond soil: This can be obtained in the garden trade. I recommend unfertilized pond compost.

Plant containers

Special plant containers for pond plants have proved to be very practical. They can be removed from the pond very easily with the help of ropes, chains or iron hooks and make care of the pond and replanting or new planting much easier. In addition, they keep vigorously growing plants in check. They are indispensable if bottom-feeding fish like goldfish or koi live in your pond. Their constant rummaging about while feeding at the bottom would soon turn a clay-rich bottom into a murky brew.

Mesh baskets: These baskets come in different sizes and are round, square or oval.

Coconut fibre: Baskets made out of coconut fibre look very natural.

Verge matting: These loosely woven mats, many of which are equipped with practical planting pockets, are ideal for planting steeper banks (see designing the edge of the pond, p. 18).

Tips on planting

Planting time: You can plant from spring right through to autumn. As pond plants are usually grown in plant containers, there is no risk of damage to roots when planting so the plants will continue to grow.

Density of plants: The general rule for initial planting is:
● four to six plants per m² (11 sq ft) in the marginal zone
● three to four plants per m² (11 sq ft) in the shallow-water zone
● for water lilies, the number will depend on speed of growth (see table, pp. 46/47)
● two to three underwater plants per m² (11 sq ft) of water surface.

My tip: Plant less rather than too much. Adding plants later on is better than having plants crowding each other.

Planting and caring for water lilies

Not every type of water lily is suited to every pond, as different varieties have different requirements with respect to planting or water depth and not all of them are hardy (see table, pp. 46/47).

Planting tip: Most water lilies have a longish, rounded rhizome that continues to grow constantly at the vegetation tip (the point where shoots of leaves and flowers are formed), while the older parts slowly die off. These rhizomes have to be laid horizontally or at a slight angle in the soil when they are planted.

Exception: The tuberous rhizome of some of the small-growing varieties is planted vertically; for example, the dwarf water lily (*Nymphea tetragona*).

NB: Water lilies planted in plant containers should be treated like pot plants.

Planting the rhizome:
I recommend planting water lilies in mesh baskets. Before planting, shorten the roots of the rhizome to about a hand's width. Cut out all decaying parts and brush all cut surfaces with charcoal powder to prevent decay.

Tips on care: Remove dead leaves and flowers with a sharp knife but only if absolutely necessary.

Overwintering: Hardy water lilies should be slid into the deep water zone. Non-hardy varieties should be taken out of the pond and placed in a cool room, covered with dead leaves. Occasionally check the rhizomes and cut out any decayed parts.

Line the mesh basket with a piece of protective plant fabric.

Fill two thirds with soil. Set the rhizome horizontally and add soil until the shoot tip is barely covered. Water well. Fold the fabric inwards.

Correct planting

Plant species: The selection of plants that can be used to decorate the bank of a pond or stream is almost infinite. Most of these marginal plants feel at home in moist soil but do not like to have their "feet" in water.

Some have special requirements with respect to soil; for example, they may need soil that contains very little lime (see plant compost, p. 38). These requirements are easily met at the edge of the pond by placing the plants in baskets or grouping them together in one position.

The plant tables on pages 42/43 provide information on requirements regarding light, soil and care of the most popular plant species that thrive in the damp bank zone of a garden pond or stream.

Purple loosestrife.

Lesser reed mace.

Umbrella grass.

Cotton grass.

Marsh forget-me-not.

A Siberian iris makes a splash of colour in the garden pond.

Protecting wild flora:
Many plants that will thrive on the edge of a pond may be found growing wild by ponds and lakes. Please do not remove whole plants, parts of plants or seed from the wild. Many plants are now protected species because they are threatened by extinction. In truth, everything that you really want can now be found in a garden centre or obtained from specialist nurseries or special water plant retailers.

Cyperus sedge.

Greenery and flowers for the edge of the pond

Japanese iris.

Creeping Jenny.

Correct planting

Name	Light	Soil/water depth	Flowering time Flowering colour	Height of growth	Special features
Ajuga reptans bugle	◑–●	loamy, humus-rich soil	LSP-ES blue, pink, white	10-30 cm (4-12 in)	Ground-covering, cannot tolerate lime, attractive foliage colour. Also along banks of streams.
Calluna vulgaris heather, ling	○	moist, slightly acid soil	LS-MA red	20-50 cm (8-20 in)	Ideal for marginal bed.
Cardamine pratensis cuckoo flower	○–●	slightly acid soil	MSP-LSP delicate lilac	up to 30 cm (up to 12 in)	Easy to propagate, plant in small groups. Also along stream bank.
Carex paniculata greater tussock-sedge	○–●	damp bank, chalky soil	LSP-ES light brown	up to 100 cm (up to 40 in)	No waterlogging, forms clumps.
Carex pendula sedge	○–◑	damp bank, slightly acid soil	LSP-ES yellow brown	40-90 cm (16-36 in)	No waterlogging, evergreen.
Carex pseudocyperus sedge	○–◑	damp bank, slightly acid soil	ES-MS yellow green	up to 100 cm (up to 40 in)	No waterlogging, solitary plant.
Cirsium palustre plume thistle	○–◑	slightly acid soil	MS-EA purple	up to 150 cm (up to 60 in)	Biennial, undemanding, much sought after by insects. Also along stream banks.
Comarum palustre	○–●	pH value 6.5 or lower	ES-MS purple	20 cm (8 in)	Ground-covering. Rhizomes up to 100 cm (40 in) long. Also along stream banks.
Dianthus superbus pink	◑	moist pond bank, slightly acid soil	ES-EA pink	30-60 cm (12-24 in)	Scented. Also along stream banks.
Eriophorum angustifolium cotton grass	○–◑	acid soil, 0-15 cm (0-6 in)	MSP-LSP white	up to 50 cm (up to 20 in)	Decorative, woolly, white seedheads.
Eriophorum latifolium cotton grass	○–◑	lime-rich soil, 0-15 cm (0-6 in)	MSP-LSP white	up to 60 cm (up to 24 in)	Decorative woolly, white seedheads. Also along stream banks. Protected!
Eupatorium cannabinum hemp agrimony	○	lime-rich soil	MS-EA dirty reddish-pink	up to 150 cm (up to 60 in)	May grow rampant, sought after by insects. Also along stream banks.
Filipendula ulmaria meadowsweet	○–◑	humus-rich and acid soil	ES-MS yellowish-white	up to 150 cm (up to 60 in)	Aromatic scented flowers, pink-flowering varieties the trade.
Gentiana asclepiadea gentian	◑	wet, humus-rich, slightly acid soil	LS-MA blue	50-80 cm (20-32 in)	Very decorative.
Geranium palustre cranesbill	◑	moist, 0-2 cm (0-½ in) neutral soil	LSP-LS lilac	30-50 cm (12-20 in)	Good for marginal beds.
Geum rivale water avens	○–◑	humus-rich and acid soil	LSP-MS reddish-brown	70 cm (28 in)	Undemanding, easy to propagate from division. Sought after by bees. Also along stream banks.
Hypericum calycinium rose of Sharon	○–◑	loam, sand	MS-LS golden yellow	30 cm (12 in)	Ground-covering, evergreen, undemanding. Also along stream banks.
Hypericum moserianum St. John's wort	◑	loam, sand	MS-MA golden yellow	30 cm (12 in)	Groundcovering, undemanding. Also along stream banks.
Impatiens noli-tangere busy Lizzie	◑	neutral, slightly acid soil	MS-EA pink to red	up to 130 cm (up to 52 in)	Easy to propagate from seed; ripe seed hurled out explosively.
Iris kaempferi Japanese iris	○	slightly acid soil	ES-MS many colours	up to 70 cm (28 in)	Varieties in many colours, plant in groups. Contains skin-irritants!
Iris sibirica iris	○–◑	slightly acid soil	LSP-ES blue violet	up to 100 cm (up to 40 in)	Forms thick carpets, cannot tolerate fertilizer. Contains skin-irritants! Protected!
Juncus rush	○–◑	slightly acid soil 0-15 cm (0-6 in)	ES-LS brown	25-80 cm (10-32 in)	Water-cleaning properties, consumes nutrients. Also in a stream. Protected!
Lasiagrostis calamagrostis	○	pond edge, humus-rich soil	ES-MA	up to 70 cm (up to 28 in)	Flowers very profusely. The silver ears turn brownish in the autumn.

Name	Light	Soil/water depth	Flowering time Flowering colour	Height of growth	Special features
Liatris spicata gayfeather	○	neutral soil	MS-MA purple, pink, white	up to 90 cm (36 in)	Undemanding, parts above ground die off in winter.
Lysimachia nummularia creeping Jenny	○ – ◐	almost dry soil, water up to 15 cm (6 in) deep	ES-MS yellow	up to 10 cm (up to 4 in)	Ground-covering, ideal for banks. Also in stream and along stream bank.
Lysimachia vulgaris yellow loosestrife	○ – ◐	neutral soil, edge of pond	ES-LS golden yellow	up to 150 cm (up to 60 in)	May grow rampant, particularly sensitive to waterlogging. Also along stream bank.
Lythrum salicaria purple loosestrife	○	neutral soil up to 40 cm (16 in)	ES-EA purple red	up to 200 cm (up to 80 in)	Not sensitive, may also stand in water, do not plant together with profusely growing plants.
Mentha longifolia horse mint	○ – ◐	neutral soil	MS-EA delicate pink	30-100 cm (12-40 in)	Not suitable for making teas. No waterlogging. Also along stream banks.
Mentha piperita peppermint	◐	neutral soil	MS-EA whitish	50-80 cm (20-32 in)	Cannot tolerate waterlogging, otherwise not sensitive. Suitable for teas.
Mentha rotundifolia round-leafed mint	◐ – ●	damp soil	MS-EA pink	30-60 cm (12-24 in)	Not sensitive. No waterlogging. Also along stream banks.
Molinia coerulea tussocky grass	○ – ◐	edge of pond, humus-rich, moist soil	MS-EA green-purple	up to 50 cm (up to 20 in)	Attractive autumn colouring. Clumps die off above ground. New shoots from mid-spring.
Myosotis palustris marsh forget-me-not	○ – ◐	slightly acid soil	LSP-EA light blue	up to 30 cm (up to 12 in)	Continuously flowering, goes well with marsh marigold. Also along stream banks.
Osmunda regalis royal fern	◐ – ●	humus-rich, acid soil	no flower	up to 120 cm (up to 48 in)	Add plenty of peat to compost, brownish colouring in autumn very attractive. Protected!
Pennisetum compressum	○	edge of pond, humus-rich moist soil	LS-MA brown	up to 70 cm (up to 28 in)	Beautiful, fluffy, brownish flower spikes. Cut back (to hand high) in spring.
Petasites hybridus butterbur	○ – ●	neutral soil	ESP-LSP pinkish-white	up to 40 cm (up to 16 in)	After flowering, up to 100 cm (40 in), proliferates wildly, regular thinning out.
Phragmites australis reed	○ – ◐	water 0-15 cm (0-6 in) deep	LS-MA purple	up to 200 cm (up to 80 in)	Important for noticeable water-cleaning properties, uses up lots of nutrients.
Potentilla palustris marsh cinquefoil	○	moist, slightly acid soil	ES-MS red	20-40 cm (8-16 in)	Ideal for marginal bed.
Primula vialii rockery primrose	◐ – ●	moist, humus-rich soil	ES-LS scarlet	up to 50 cm (up to 20 in)	Continuously flowering, plant in large groups.
Sasa palmata	○ – ◐	edge of pond, humus-rich soil	MA-LA	80-150 cm (32-60 in)	Grows densely, also ground-covering. Also along stream banks.
Schoenoplectus tabernaemontani	○ – ◐	water 0-30 cm (0-12 in) deep	LS brownish	up to 70 cm (up to 28 in)	Undemanding, water-cleaning. Also in a stream.
Sinarundinaria nitida	○ – ◐	edge of pond, moist, humus-rich soil	LS-MA	up to 250 cm (up to 100 in)	Hardy, still requires some winter protection with dead leaves around the plant. Can be pruned.
Stachys palustris marsh woundwort	○ – ◐	edge of pond, moist humus	ES-EA purple	30-100 cm (12-40 in)	Not demanding. Also along stream banks.
Symphytum officinale common comfrey	○ – ◐	neutral soil	LSP-MS red violet, yellowish-white	up to 120 cm (up to 48 in)	Easy to propagate from seed, no problems, second flowering through radical cutting back.
Thelypteris palustris	○ – ●	acid soil	no flower	up to 80 cm (up to 32 in)	With glowing, light green fronds, easy to propagate from division.
Trollius europaeus globeflower ☠	○ – ●	slightly acid soil	LSP-ES yellow	up to 60 cm (up to 24 in)	Delicately scented. Sought after by honey bees and bumble bees. Protected!
Typha angustifolia reedmace	○	water 0-50 cm (0-20 in) deep	MS-LS	50-180 cm (20-72 in)	Water-cleaning, competes with algae, *Typha minima*. Also along banks. Protected!

Plants for a pond

It is important, both for the quality of the water in the pond and for the inhabitants of the pond, that plants from each of the following groups are represented in the garden pond.

Marginal plants: Only the roots or lower portions are submerged in water. They are planted in shallow water, in the marginal zone and in the damp soil along the edges of the pond.

Surface plants: They root in the soil, their leaves and flowers have long stalks and float on the surface. They are happy in water 30-40 cm (12-16 in) deep.

Floating plants: They have more or less developed roots and the whole plant floats freely on the surface of the water. Occasionally these plants need to be thinned out.

Submerged oxygenating plants: They live under the water. In a few species only the leaves protrude above the surface of the water. They have an important function in a garden pond as they produce oxygen and absorb minerals, carbon dioxide and the metabolic waste products of fish. This puts them in direct competition with algae and helps to keep the latter in check. During the summer, thin the plants out occasionally, particularly in small ponds.

The pink water lily "Pink Sensation".

Brilliant yellow water fringe.

Water lilies: Water lilies flower more luxuriantly and earlier if you do not place the water lily baskets in the depth of water that is recommended for them but, instead, proceed in the following manner:

● Place the basket in shallow water.

● When the leaves begin to rise above the surface of the water, slide the basket down into deeper water until the leaves are just submerged.

● Repeat this process until the basket ends up in the prescribed position.

Other possibilities: Pile up perforated bricks in the final position of the basket until the basket is sitting in a shallow-water position. Then gradually lower the basket by taking away one brick at a time.

Fertilizing tip: Add 1 tablespoon of hoof/horn chips to each water lily basket every time you plant or replant it.

Arrowhead.

Mare's tail.

Common bladderwort.

Correct planting

Name	Light	Zone/depth of water	Flowering time Flowering colour	Height of growth	Special features
Acorus calamus sweet flag	○	0-25 cm (0-10 in)	LSP-MS yellow green, inconspicuous	to 120 cm (to 48 in)	Undemanding, proliferating, propagation only from division. Contains skin-irritants!
Alisma plantago-aquatica water plantain	○ – ◐	0-25 cm (0-10 in)	ES-LS white	to 80 cm (32 in)	Consumes nutrients, proliferates, divide rootstock after two years. Also in stream.
Aponogeton distachyos water hawthorn	○	from 30 cm (from 12 in)	ESP-MA white	surface plant	Flowers smell of vanilla, grow young plants in shallow water, care as for water lilies.
Azolla caroliana fairy moss	○ – ●	from 30 cm (from 12 in)	no flower	floating plant	Keeps algae in check, overwinter in a flat dish in bright, cool position.
Butomus umbellatus flowering rush	○	0-25 cm (0-10 in)	ES-LS pinkish-white	to 120 cm (to 48 in)	Must stand in water, plant together with irises. Also in stream.
Calla palustris bog arum	○ – ●	0-25 cm (0-10 in)	LSP-MS green	to 40 cm (to 16 in)	Requires slightly acid soil. Fruit (red berries) are toxic! Top leaf=white/flower=yellowish.
Callitriche palustris water starwort	○ – ●	30-60 cm (12-24 in)	MSP-MA inconspicuous	surface plant	Remains green during winter, provides oxygen even under ice. Also in stream.
Caltha palustris marsh marigold	○ – ●	0-25 cm (0-10 in)	MSP-ES golden yellow	to 20 cm (to 8 in)	Undemanding. Forms cushions, roots must be able to reach water. Also beside stream.
Ceratophyllum demersum hornwort	○	from 30 cm (from 12 in)	no flower	submerged oxygenating plant	Very feathery plant without roots, cannot tolerate peat.
Eichhornia crassipes water hyacinth	○	from 30 cm (from 12 in)	LS-EA light violet	floating plant	Will only flower if water temperature is above 20°C (68°F). Overwinter in an aquarium.
Elodea, Egeria canadensis Canadian pondweed	○	from 30 cm (from 12 in)	LSP-LS white	submerged oxygenating plant	Rarely flowers; propagation only from stalk sections. Also in stream.
Epilobium hirsutum great willowherb	○	0-5 cm (0-2 in)	ES-EA purple pink	90-120 cm (36-48 in)	For natural banks; requires severe cutting back. Also in streams and stream banks.
Gratiola officinalis	○	0-5 cm (0-2 in)	ES-LS white or pink	20-40 cm (8-16 in)	Cannot tolerate peat, otherwise undemanding. Also in stream.
Hippuris vulgaris mare's tail	○	0-25 cm (0-10 in)	LSP-LS greenish, small	to 200 cm (to 80 in)	Flower stalk protrudes above water's surface, not easy to grow, soft water. Also in stream.
Hottonia palustris water violet	○	0-40 cm (0-16 in)	LSP-MS white to violet pink	30-50 cm (12-20 in)	Protected!
Hydrocharis morsus ranae frog bit	○	from 30 cm (from 12 in)	ES-LS white	floating plant	Cannot tolerate lime, easy to propagate from rosettes. Protected!
Iris pseudacorus common flag	○ – ●	0-25 cm (0-10 in)	LSP-LS yellow	to 80 cm (32 in)	Set in water in baskets, attracts dragonflies. Leaves and stalks contain toxins!
Lemna minor duckweed	○	from 30 cm (from 12 in)	no flower	floating plant	Keeps algae in check, remove regularly during summer months, prune severely in autumn.
Ligularia tangutica golden rays	○ – ●	0-8 cm (0-3 in)	MS-EA yellow	80-120 cm (32-48 in)	Decorative, grows fast. Requires acid soil.
Mentha aquatica water mint	○ – ●	0-25 cm (0-10 in)	MS-MA light violet	to 80 cm (to 32 in)	Aromatic scent, easy to grow, proliferates. Also in stream.
Menyanthes trifoliata bog bean	○ – ●	to 25 cm (to 10 in)	LSP-ES red	to 30 cm (to 12 in)	Requires slightly acid soil. Protected!
Myriophyllum spicatum water milfoil	○	from 30 cm (from 12 in)	MS-EA pale pink	submerged oxygenating plant	Flower spike about 15 cm (6 in) above water, propagation from stalk or winter buds.
Nuphar lutea yellow water lily	○ – ●	30-200 cm (12-40 in)	ES-LS eggyolk yellow	surface plant	Requires sandy bottom. Dwarf lilies (*Nuphar pumila*) better for small ponds. Protected!

Name	Light	Zone/depth of water	Flowering time Flowering colour	Height of growth	Special features
Nymphaea alba white water lily	○–◐	from 30 cm (from 12 in)	LSP-LS white	surface plant	Indigenous white water lily, strictly protected, buy only cultivated plants, many cultivars.
Nymphaea spp. dwarf water lilies	○–◐	15-30 cm (6-12 in)	LSP-MA many colours	surface plant	Overwinter in deep water zone or in a cool room.
Nymphaea spp. medium-fast-growing water lilies	○–◐	40-70 cm (16-28 in)	LSP-MA many colours	surface plant	Fully grown, a plant covers an area of about 1 m² (11 sq ft).
Nymphaea spp. fast-growing water lilies	○–◐	70-100 cm (28-40 in)	LSP-LA many colours	surface plant	For ponds from about 6 m² (65 sq ft), one plant requires about 2 m² (22 sq ft) water surface area.
Nymphaea spp. very fast-growing warer lilies	○–◐	more than 100 cm (over 40 in)	LSP-MA many colours	surface plant	Only for very large ponds, 3-4 m² (32-43 sq ft) area to spread per plant.
Nymphoides peltata water fringe	○–◐	40-50 cm (16-20 in)	ES-LS brilliant yellow	surface plant	Proliferates, remove nine-tenths in autumn, ideal for raising fish. Protected!
Pistia stratiotes water lettuce	○	from 30 cm (from 12 in)	no flower	floating plant	Controls algae, water temperatures above 15°C (59°F), overwinter in an aquarium.
Polygonum amphibium amphibious bistort	○–◐	0-50 cm (0-20 in)	ES-EA pink	up to 30 cm (12 in)	Undemanding, proliferates, consumes nutrients. The leaves contain skin-irritants! Also in stream.
Potamogeton pondweed	○–◐	from 30 cm (from 12 in)	ES-LS inconspicuous	surface plant	In pond and stream, oxygenator, water-cleaning, checks algae, hiding place for young fish.
Primula denticulata drumstick primula	◐	0-5 cm (0-2 in)	MSP-LSP many colours	20-40 cm (8-16 in)	In the autumn, reduce water level. Requires slightly acid soil.
Ranunculus aquatilis water crowfoot	○–◐	30-60 cm (12-24 in)	LSP-LS white	surface plant	Keeps algae in check, regularly thin out, remove foliage in autumn. Also in stream.
Ranunculus lingua great spearwort	○	0-25 cm (0-10 in)	ES-LS golden yellow	up to 70 cm (28 in)	Grows under water in winter, undemanding, oxygenator. Also in stream. Protected!
Rumex aquaticus Scottish dock	○–◐	0-15 cm (0-6 in)	ES-MS pinkish	50-60 cm (20-24 in)	Consumes nitrogen, keeps algae in check. Also in stream.
Sagittaria sagittifolia arrowhead	○	0-25 cm (0-10 in)	ES-LS white	up to 40 cm (16 in)	Undemanding, competes with algae, oxygenator. Tubers contain skin-irritants! Also in stream.
Salvinia natans	○–◐	from 30 cm (from 12 in)	no flower	floating plant	Controls algae, remove chunks occasionally, requires warmth, propagates from spores.
Sparganium erectum branched bur-reed	○–◐	0-25 cm (0-10 in)	ES-LS greenish	up to 120 cm (48 in)	Will also thrive in deep water, undemanding, regularly shorten roots. Also in stream.
Stratiotes aloides water soldier	○	from 30 cm (from 12 in)	LSP-LS white	floating plant	Water cleaning, use to stop growth of algae, easy to propagate from rosettes, protected!
Saururus cernuus lizard's tail	○–◐	0-30 cm (0-12 in)	MS-LS neutral	80-100 cm (32-40 in)	Sensitive to frost. Requires neutral soil.
Trapa natans water chestnut	○–◐	30-70 cm (12-28 in)	ES-EA white	surface plant	Consumes nutrients, parent plant dies in autumn, seeds overwinter in pond. Protected!
Utricularia vulgaris common bladderwort	○	from 30 cm (from 12 in)	ES-LS golden yellow	submerged oxygenating plant	Flower stalk protrudes above water, carnivorous plant (plankton), helps to control *Volvox*.
Veronica beccabunga brooklime	○–◐	0-25 cm (0-10 in)	LSP-MA blue	up to 30 cm (12 in)	Forms cushions, creeping growth, prefers hard water, cannot tolerate peat. Also in stream.
Veronica longifolia	●	0-5 cm (0-2 in)	ES-LS blue	80-100 cm (32-40 in)	Decorative, for marginal bed. Requires slightly acid soil.
Zizania aquatica	○–◐	10-30 cm (4-12 in)	MS-EA	80-100 cm (32-40 in)	Edible. Also in stream.

Care and overwintering

One of the good things about a garden pond is that it creates relatively little work over a whole year. The measures of care that are necessary to maintain pond life throughout the year should, however, be carried out faithfully. Among these is making sure that certain tasks are carried out in autumn to help the pond to get through the winter.

Above: A frog is a popular visitor to a pond.
Left: A large pond with a summer house and a walkway leading to it.

Care and overwintering

Care all year round

The largest amount of work connected with a pond is building it and stocking it with plants. Over the following years you will, as a rule, have little work and lots of pleasure.

Summer: only a few duties.

● When necessary, exchange the water or top up.

● Check water values (see below), so that you will be able to deal quickly with deteriorating water quality.

● Thin out very vigorously growing plants.

● Feed fish and watch their behaviour. A change in behaviour may indicate disease (see p. 52).

Autumn: This is the time to prepare the pond for the winter (see pp. 54/55).

Winter: This is the rest period for a pond; all life processes slow right down. Any disturbance now would harm the pond inhabitants.

Warning: Never smash a hole in an ice sheet. The pond creatures, fish in particular, would be greatly harmed by the shock and vibration.

Spring: The first warm rays of sunlight slowly wake the pondlife. From the beginning of spring you can start to get the pond ready for summer.

● Check all around the edge of the pond. Damage to the banks can be put right. Clean out the soakaway.

● Check that all appliances (filter, pump) are functioning properly; try them out.

● Test the water and regulate if necessary (see below).

● During early spring, add plants if required and, at intervals of a week a time, gradually lower water lilies to their final position (see pp. 44/45).

● Feed fish as soon as the water temperature reaches 12°C (54°F).

Warning: Do not transfer fish that have overwintered in an aquarium into the pond until the difference in temperature between the aquarium and pond water is only a few degrees Fahrenheit.

Checking and improving the water quality

Three vital water values play an important part in maintaining the balance of the complicated life processes in a pond. These are the degree of acidity, the nitrite-nitrate content and water hardness. If one of these values gets out of balance, it can result in dire consequences for the quality of the water and for the pond inhabitants.

You should occasionally measure these values so that you can take action immediately (especially important if fish live in the pond). You can obtain reagents in the form of testing strips that are very easy to use, as well as various other aids, from garden centres or aquarium retailers who will also be able to advise you on their use and how to overcome specific problems.

The acidity of the water

This value is expressed as the pH factor. This provides information as to whether the water is neutral (pH 7), acidic (pH 0-6.9) or alkaline (pH 7.1-14). The following applies for both water and soil:

acid = lime content low
alkaline = contains lime.

Fish can cope with pH values of 6.5-8.5 (slightly acid to slightly alkaline). Values below pH 6 may endanger fish; values around pH 5 are generally lethal.

Measuring the pH should be carried out with other routine measurements (about every six to eight weeks) in the summer, especially after heavy showers of rain (possibly polluted or acid rain), and in the autumn when lots of leaves fall into the water. Both rain and leaves can rapidly push the pH value to dangerous levels.

pH values that are too low can be corrected by *slowly* exchanging one third of the water. Repeat if necessary.

pH values that are too high can be lowered by hanging a sackful of pond peat in the water until the desired value is obtained.
NB: Check regularly as the pH value must not drop too low!
NB: Short-term fluctuations of the pH value are normal and will not harm fish.

The nitrite-nitrate content

Dead parts of plants and waste from animals (excrement) are broken down by bacteria. During this process, nitrites are formed which are toxic to fish but these are then further transformed into harmless nitrates. During this constant process of transformation, oxygen is absorbed from the water. As long as sufficient oxygen is present in the water and the amounts of debris contained in the water are not too great (nutrient excess), the process will continue without problems. The nitrite-nitrate content will remain low and will not influence the well-being of the fish.
Too high a nitrite-nitrate content: This will harm the fish and disturb the entire pond. The result is increased growth of algae and symptoms of toxicosis in fish. Lack of oxygen will drive the fish to the surface where they will gasp for air (emergency respiration).
Prevention: Exchange one third

of the water every three weeks and do not overfeed the fish.
In an emergency, particularly if the fish are already gasping for air, add oxygen, exchange one third of the water and add a water preparation agent to the water when filling up.

Hardness

The total hardness of water is measured in degrees Clark. The degrees of hardness are determined as follows:
● 5-10 degrees Clark = soft water
● 10-21 degrees Clark = medium-hard water
● 22-38 degrees Clark = hard water.
Advice on the degree of hardness of your water can be obtained from your local water authority or you can test it yourself with the relevant reagent testing aid from an aquarium supplier.
Medium-hard water is *suitable for fish.*
Carbonate hardness is a separate measurement. Reagents for measuring this can also be obtained from aquarium retailers. This measurement is important as the carbonate hardness determines to what extent fluctuations of pH values can be regulated so that they do not develop to extremes that would be lethal for many pond inhabitants.

Controlling the water levels

By using an ordinary plastic toilet cistern, you can ensure that water is automatically topped up when low.
Installation: The cistern should be attached to an L-shaped block in such a way that the ballcock can move up and down. (Adjust the level of the ballcock arm until the ballcock floats at the desired level.) A strong pipe should connect the device to the water mains.
Function: When the water level drops, the ballcock will drop down and a valve will open and let fresh water into the pond. Once the correct water level has been reached, the ballcock will rise and the valve will close.

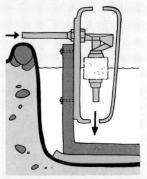

The cistern should be open at the top and bottom.

Care and overwintering

These colourful koi require clean, oxygen-rich water.

Goldfish – the classic pond fish

Goldfish in your garden pond will prove to be equally fascinating for young and old alike.

Care: Goldfish are undemanding creatures that will thrive even in small ponds (minimum 3 m²/32 sq ft water surface area) if their basic requirements of food, clean water and sufficient oxygen are met. This means that you will need to install a filtering device and probably also an air pump or oxygenator to supply additional oxygen to a goldfish pond. These colourful fish eat both plant and animal food and would soon turn the pondwater into a bad-smelling brew and probably also expire themselves without some of these helpful aids.

Goldfish.

The fish: The popular and well-adapted common goldfish (*Carassius auratus*) comes in a range of beautiful colours (red, gold, orange, bronze, white with gold and black with gold). Of the many hybrids that have been raised, only the following are suitable for continuous life in a garden pond: shubunkins, comets and fantails. Other hybrids can only be kept in a garden pond under certain conditions and are best kept by experienced fish keepers. Precise information on keeping and caring for goldfish can be found in specialist literature.

Initial stock: Choose a variety of goldfish but not too many as they will soon multiply.

My tip: Place plants in the pond in mesh baskets (see p. 38). Goldfish like to feed on the pond floor and would soon churn up the bottom so that the water becomes murky.

Koi – the princes among pond fish

Koi (Japanese carp) are extremely handsome fish. They are also fairly expensive but, despite this, are becoming ever more popular among enthusiastic garden pond owners. If you wish to keep two or three of these beauties, you should purchase a specialist book on the subject and read it thoroughly before making your choice. In this guide there is room for only a few notes on correct care.

Care: Clean, oxygen-rich water is among the basic requirements of these handsome fish. They are considerably more demanding than goldfish. As koi can grow up to 60 cm (2 ft) long, the pond should not be any smaller than 10 m² (108 sq ft); 15² m (160 sq ft) would be even better. The deep-water zone should measure at least 1 m² (11 sq ft) and have a depth of 1.5-1.8 m (5-6 ft) if the koi have to overwinter in the pond.

The fish: Koi can be obtained from aquarium retailers or specialist dealers. Their price will depend on the quality of the stock but they will not be cheap.

Indigenous fish

Indigenous fish that can be kept in small ponds combine both beauty and usefulness. Many of them will help to control insects and algae.

● The favourite food of the golden orfe, a variety of the orfe (*Leuciscus idus*) is the troublesome mosquito.

● The gudgeon (*Gobio gobio*) will eat dragonfly larvae and the larvae of the great diving beetle.

● *Leucaspius delineatus* will eat flying insects and bits of algae.

● The grass carp (*Ctenopharyngodon idella*) attacks filamentous algae.

Care: Indigenous fish will feel quite at home in a well-cared-for garden pond. Keep fish like golden orfe in a small shoal of at least ten individuals.

My tip: Do not put too many fish in your garden pond as it will not be good for either the fish or the pond.

Warning: Remember that a pond containing fish will prove a great attraction to both children and predators such as cats and birds. You must make sure that children do not attempt to catch the fish or frighten them by dropping objects in the water. A grid just under the surface or large-leaved water foliage should help to keep the fish safe from predators. You must also make sure that small children and dogs cannot climb or fall into the pond as this could prove dangerous for all concerned.

Tips on feeding

Fish rapidly become accustomed to regular feeding. As soon as anyone approaches the pond, they will gather in a group and pretend they are just about on the point of starvation. This should not tempt you to give them food every time. The fish will not starve as there is usually a whole range of natural food for them in a properly built and maintained pond.

Care and overwintering

Overfrequent feeding and the wrong kind of food may lead to a rapid deterioration of the quality of the water.

Please make sure that you and your children observe the following points:

● Give only food that has been specially prepared for garden pond fish (bought from aquarium retailers).

● I recommend flaked food in the spring and autumn as it does not leave too much detritus floating in the water.

● During the summer, you should feed a pelleted mixture specially produced for pond fish (obtainable from aquarium retailers and garden centres).

● Koi require special food bought from aquarium suppliers.

● It is essential that you only give them as much food as they can consume within five minutes.

● Those fish species that prefer animal food should occasionally be given live food. This is sold fresh or frozen by aquarium retailers.

● Dry bread and kitchen refuse of any kind are harmful to the fish and the pond.

NB: In the autumn, gradually switch to flaked food and then gradually cease feeding altogether once the temperature drops to 12°C (54°F). Even if the fish are still feeding, they will find the food difficult to digest. In the spring, start feeding with flakes again when the temperature reaches 15°C (59°F).

Preparing an ornamental pond for the winter

Once the fish have stopped feeding at a water temperature of 12°C (54°F), winter has begun in your garden pond. Before the ornamental pond settles into its long winter sleep, there are a few things for you to do so that your fish and plants will survive the winter.

The aim of the autumn clear out is not a radically cleaned pond in which there is no longer any trace of useful micro-organisms. Autumn cleaning is done so that, during the winter rest period, nothing is left quietly decaying as this would result in oxygen deficiency, the production of unwelcome gases, excess nutrients and a dramatic deterioration in water quality.

Work around the pond

● Pull out the plugs of all electrical appliances.

● Allow a good two thirds of the pond water to drain out.

● Carefully lift out plant baskets.

● Gently catch the fish and place them in a large tub that was previously filled with pondwater. Cover this with a cloth so that the fish cannot jump out.

● Place amphibians that live near the pond in a safe, sheltered place. They will usually return to the water by themselves later on. If they do not you should put them back in the pond carefully.

● Remove most of the sludge at the bottom of the pond that is made up of decayed plant remains and other debris.

If they are present, gather up the seeds of water chestnuts (*Trapa natans*) and return them to the pond later on, preferably in a water lily basket.

Plant care before the winter

Rotting plants will absorb too much oxygen from your ornamental pond so they should be radically reduced. This will not harm the plants and they will all start shooting again in the spring.

● Floating plants and submerged oxygenating plants should be radically thinned out.

● Vigorously proliferating plants should be well cut back.

Exception: reed mace, rushes, reeds, sedges and grasses. These plants should not be cut back until the spring as they are useful oxygen suppliers in the winter and also provide protection for many small creatures.

● Remove dead and torn plant matter from the pond.

● Scrub algae off the edges of the pond with a stiff brush.

● Transplant water lilies now if you wish. Cut off leaves, flowers and stalks but do not remove the leaf and flower buds! Shorten the rhizomes by a third, remove all decayed parts, replant the rhizomes in larger baskets if necessary. Hardy species should be placed in the deepest part of the pond. Non-hardy species should be placed in a cool, frost-free room and covered with dead leaves. Check regularly and remove any rotting parts immediately.

Run in fresh water: After all these jobs have been carried out, allow fresh water, together with water preparation agents (from aquarium retailers or garden centres), to run slowly back into the pond.

Fish: You can gently place them back in the pond provided the deep water zone is more than 60 cm (2 ft) deep. Otherwise, the fish should be overwintered in an aquarium.

Coping with ice

A typical ice-preventer.

An ice-preventer of a more unusual design.

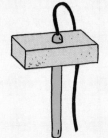

The pond heater should be equipped with a sufficiently long cable.

You will be able to keep a permanent hole in the ice on the surface of the pond if you use a special gadget or a pond heater.

Ice-preventer: A reliable, cheap aid that is very easy to operate. This gadget is made of polystyrene. It is placed on the surface of the water and anchored in a deep part of the pond. It will work up to -20°C (-4°F). Follow the manufacturer's instructions.

Pond heater: The name is a little misleading. The device does not actually heat the pond but simply keeps a hole free of ice in the ice sheet on top of the pond using a few watts of electricity. It requires an electrical connection. Switch the heater on when the temperature reaches freezing and off again when the ice thaws. If the heater should get frozen in, do not hack it out but simply switch it on again! **NB:** It will also help if the oxygen pump is left running continuously.

Warning: Never, ever use an aquarium heater in a pond! Never, ever use an extension cable!

Care and overwintering

Only very large, natural ponds with a surface area of more than 30 m² (323 sq ft) can be left to overwinter without any preparation.

In the case of small ponds, a few tidying up jobs are required or else the pond would become completely choked with weed and debris after a few years. Allow a third of the water to run out slowly and also let the fresh water run in slowly. Care for the plants is as described for an ornamental pond and will do no harm if you proceed gently.

An oxygen supply in winter

In both summer and winter, oxygen is essential for all life in the pond. Even when the pond settles into its winter sleep at a temperature of 1°C (34°F), the life processes it contains will continue at a greatly reduced rate. At this time a dangerous lack of oxygen may occur if precautions are not taken beforehand. An additional supply of oxygen will be necessary, particularly:
● if a large stock of fish overwinter in a covered pond
● if the pond has not been covered and freezes up as soon as the temperature drops below freezing.
My tip: Always make sure that a hole is kept open in the ice sheet all winter long (see p. 55).

Oxygenator: This is a practical device for providing an additional supply of oxygen. It operates without a cable or hose (see photograph, p. 12). When the device is empty – in winter, after about three months – it will bob up to the surface and will then have to be refilled according to the manufacturer's instructions.
Oxygen pump: This pump will enrich the water with oxygen. It is particularly useful for smaller ponds (i.e. 6-8 m²/65-86 sq ft). The best place to hang an oxygen pump is in a sheltered room (house, cellar, shed) and then draw the air hose through a PVC pipe to the pond.
● Convey the air hose to a medium-deep point in the pond. The deepest point is not suitable as it would cause a strong current in the pond that would prove stressful for the fish and cause them to lose weight.
● Fix a ceramic outlet to the end of the air hose in the pond.

Covering up the pond

In regions with very cold, frosty winters, it is worth providing a cover for the pond, particularly in the case of small ponds (i.e. 6 m²/65 sq ft or less) in which fish and water lilies are overwintering.
You will need a transparent material for the cover, for example Perspex (obtainable from DIY centres). This comes in corrugated sheets that can be spread across the pond over a latticed frame made of roof battens (24 x 48 mm/1-2 in thick).
The cover should be placed sloping from north to south (erect a support made of perforated bricks at the north side).
NB: Conduct oxygen into the pond during the winter by means of an air pump or an oxygenator (see above). Regularly remove snow from the cover.

Dragonflies are among the most frequent visitors to a pond. Their larvae develop in the pond.

Visitors to the pond

The garden pond, its marginal zone and a stream will provide food and shelter for many animals. You can encourage these guests by designing the area around the pond in such a way that it is suitable for various creatures such as amphibians, for example frogs, newts and toads, birds and insects. Provide shelter such as a heap of brushwood made of twigs, with dead leaves or grass cuttings on top. Even a small heap of stones or rotting wood in a corner of the garden will ensure that many fascinating visitors appear at your pond. Remember to provide a "ladder" or other means of access and exit for small creatures. A piece of sloping wood, firmly fixed, will do.

A pond newt.

Index

Index

Author's notes

This volume mentions various electrical appliances which can be used in the care of garden ponds. When using them, always remember that any electrical installation should always be carried out by an expert. Included among these jobs is the installation of electrical connections as well the laying of electric cables. Protect yourself and others from harm by making your pond safe with a protective fence or grid if small children live in or visit your household or if the pond is not out of bounds within a fenced-off part of the garden. Taking out insurance cover specifically relating to the pond is particularly recommended. Every garden pond owner has a duty to make sure that no water, either above or under the ground, can run on to a neighbouring property. Check the water lines regularly and carry out work like an exchange of water or emptying the pond in the proper manner.

Acknowledgements

The author and publishers would like to thank Firma Heissner GmbH, Pond Technology, 36339 Lauterbach, for providing the photograph for p. 29 bottom right.

Photographer Jürgen Becker and the publishers also wish to thank the following garden owners: Garten Ven den Zwan/NL-Bergen; Design: H. Weijers/NL-Haarlem.
Garten Frucht - Schäfer/Bochum, Germany; Design: R. Bodeker/Mettmann, Germany
Garten Grimm/Düsseldorf, Germany;
Design: V. & H. Püschel/Mettmann, Germany.
Garten Goebel/Holland;
Design: H. Weijers.
Garten Noll/Mettmann, Germany; Design: V. & H. Püschel.
Garten Hartenfeller/Mettmann, Germany; Design:
V. & H. Püschel.
Garten Van Steeg/NL-Dinxperlo; Design: P. Oudolf/NL-Hummelo.

Useful address

Verge matting can be difficult to obtain. If you experience difficulties, the German firm of
OBI Martinstried-Planegg
Lena-Christ Strasse 54
82152 München
Germany
Tel: 089/85 69 84-20
Fax: 089/85 69 84-21 should be able to give you the name of a UK supplier.

Cover photographs

Front cover: *Reeds and flowering lilies decorate an ornamental pond.*
Back cover: *Pink sensation*

Photographic acknowledgements

Angermayer/Pfletschinger: p. 1 right; Becker: front cover, p. 4/5, 16/17, 21, 24 top, bottom, 28, 29 top, bottom left, bottom centre, 33 top, bottom, 37 right, 48/49; Heissner: p. 29 bottom right; Kahl: p. 1 centre left, 52 top, bottom, inside back cover, centre top; Krahmer: p. 49 right, 57 bottom; *Mein Schöner Garten*/Jarosch: p. 12 top, centre bottom, 13 top, bottom, 62 top left; *Mein Schöner Garten*/Wähner: p. 9 bottom; *Mein Schöner Garten*/Wetterwald: p. 63 left; Nickig: p. 9 top, 17 right, 36/37; Reinhard: p. 62 bottom left; Sammer: p. 63 centre bottom, top right, bottom right; Stork: p. 1 left; Strauss: inside front cover, p. 1 centre right, 5 right, 40 top left, bottom left, centre right, bottom right, 41 centre, bottom left, bottom right, 44, 45 top, 45 bottom left, bottom right, 62 top right, bottom, back cover; Wothe: p. 57 top; Zeller: p. 40 top right, 41 top, 45 bottom centre.

This edition published 1996 by Merehurst Limited
Ferry House, 51-57 Lacy Road, Putney, London SW15 1PR

© 1992 Gräfe und Unzer GmbH, Munich

ISBN 1 85391 593 9

English text copyright © Merehurst Limited 1996
Translated by Astrid Mick
Edited by Lesley Young
Design and typesetting by Paul Cooper Design
Printed in Hong Kong by Wing King Tong

Pumps and some species of plants, such as pondweeds (3) and water lilies (4), are important providers of oxygen and help to combat the invasion of algae.

1

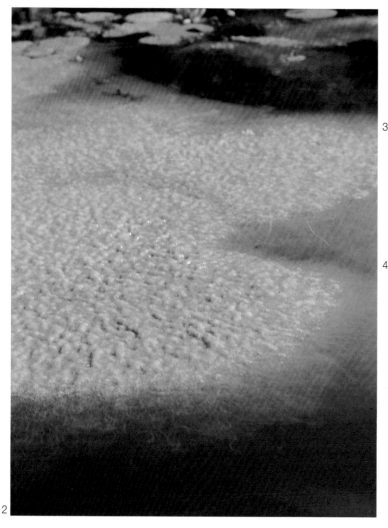

2

3

4

Combating algae without toxins

Algae are as much a part of pond life as other plants as long as they do not take over. If algae start appearing in masses, check whether you made a mistake when building the pond or are providing inadequate care. **Warning:** Never combat algae with chemical agents. These toxins only get rid of algae growth temporarily.

Recognising and dealing with problems

5 *A hole in the liner*
A pond repair kitt is now available so that small leaks can be repaired on dry surfaces and even under water. Clean the liner thoroughly with a rag, spread adhesive on the material provided as a patch and press it down hard on the damaged spot.

6 *Emergency respiration in fish*
If fish start appearing at the surface, gasping for air, this means that there could be a massive deterioration in the quality of the water (oxygen deficiency, excess nutrients).
Remedy: Change the water, add extra oxygen (see chapter on care, p. 48).

7 *Problems with fallen leaves*
Large quantities of dead leaves in a pond result in a dangerous increase in the nitrite-nitrate content and cause the pH value to drop to harmful levels.
Remedy: Remove leaves, exchange one third of the water and add a water preparation agent for three days in a row.

8 *Damage to the leaves of water lilies*
Water lily beetles and their larvae cause damage by eating the leaves.
Remedy: Remove damaged leaves and hose down the remaining leaves. Collect any pests (batches of eggs, larvae, caterpillars).
9 *Fish out algae* with a large net.

Other titles available in the series

Success with
Fuchsias

Success with
Your
Garden Pond

Success with
Bonsai

Success with
Hanging Baskets & Containers

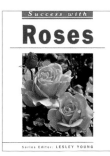
Success with
Roses

Success with
Herbs

Success with
Orchids

Success with
Climbing Plants

Success with
Geraniums
and Pelargoniums

Success with
Camellias

Success with
Cacti

Success with
Spring Flowers

Series Editor: LESLEY YOUNG